121 NEW ZEALAND POEMS

121 NEW ZEALAND POEMS

CHOSEN BY BILL MANHIRE

GODWIT

National Library of New Zealand Cataloguing-in-Publication Data
121 New Zealand poems / by 100 New Zealand poets
/ chosen by Bill Manhire.
Includes index.
ISBN 1-86962-114-X
Previous ed. published as: 100 New Zealand Poems
/ by 100 New Zealand poets. 1993.
1. New Zealand poetry. I. Manhire, Bill, 1946- II.
Title: 100 New Zealand poems.
NZ821-dc 22

A GODWIT BOOK
published by
Random House New Zealand
18 Poland Road, Glenfield, Auckland, New Zealand
www.randomhouse.co.nz

First published 2005

© 2005 Selection, Introduction and Notes: Bill Manhire; poems as credited on page 254.

The moral rights of the author have been asserted

ISBN 1 86962 114 X

Text design: Katy Yiakmis
Cover design: Dexter Fry
Cover photograph: TRANZ/Corbis
Author photo: Robert Cross
Printed in Australia by Griffin Press

contents

introduction

1: Anon. / CHARM
2: Cilla McQueen / LIVING HERE
3: Anon. / A YOUNG WOMAN FORSAKEN BY HER LOVER
4: Chris Orsman / GHOST SHIPS
5: Anon. / DAVID LOWSTON
6: Anon. / THE MARRIED ANTIPODES
7: James Edward Fitzgerald / THE NIGHT WATCH SONG OF THE 'CHARLOTTE JANE'
8: John Barr of Craigielee / THERE'S NAE PLACE LIKE OTAGO YET
9: Fiona Farrell / CHARLOTTE O'NEIL'S SONG
10: Ruth Dallas / PIONEER WOMAN WITH FERRETS
11: Jessie Mackay / THE CHARGE AT PARIHAKA
12: W.H. Oliver / PARIHAKA
13: Arthur H. Adams / THE DWELLINGS OF OUR DEAD
14: David McKee Wright / OUR CITIES FACE THE SEA
15: Dinah Hawken / THE TUG OF WAR
16: Thomas Bracken / NOT UNDERSTOOD
17: Peter Bland / BEGINNINGS: GUTHRIE SMITH IN NEW ZEALAND 1885
18: Anne Glenny Wilson / A SPRING AFTERNOON IN NEW ZEALAND
19: William Charles Hodgson / THE LAY OF THE WEATHER-BOUND
20: William Satchell / SONG OF THE GUMFIELD
21: Blanche Baughan / THE OLD PLACE
22: Henry Lawson / THE WINDY HILLS O' WELLINGTON
23: Kevin Ireland / THE FIRST TRIBUTE
24: Lloyd Jones / HOW WE THINK
25: Arnold Wall / THE CITY FROM THE HILLS
26: John Gallas / ANZAC SNAP
27: Katherine Mansfield / TO L.H.B.
28: Ursula Bethell / RESPONSE
29: R.A.K. Mason / OLD MEMORIES OF EARTH

30: Eileen Duggan / THE BUSHFELLER
31: Una Currie / TREES
32: Denis Glover / THE MAGPIES
33: A.R.D. Fairburn / WALKING ON MY FEET
34: Bub Bridger / JOHNNY COME DANCING
35: Charles Brasch / THE ISLANDS
36: J.R. Hervey / SHE WAS MY LOVE WHO COULD DELIVER
37: Robin Hyde / from THE BEACHES
38: Donald McDonald / TIME
39: Janet Frame / A NOTE ON THE RUSSIAN WAR
40: Bruce Stronach / LAST RUN
41: William Hart-Smith / SUBJECT MATTER
42: Mary Stanley / THE WIFE SPEAKS
43: Rachel McAlpine / BEFORE THE FALL
44: Peter Cape / TAUMARUNUI
45: Joe Charles / BLACK BILLY TEA
46: Hone Tuwhare / MONOLOGUE
47: M.K. Joseph / SECULAR LITANY
48: Mary / TELEPHONE WIRES
49: Keith Sinclair / THE BOMB IS MADE
50: Louis Johnson / SONG IN THE HUTT VALLEY
51: Kendrick Smithyman / COLVILLE 1964
52: Fleur Adcock / FOR A FIVE-YEAR-OLD
53: Vincent O'Sullivan / DON'T KNOCK THE RAWLEIGH'S MAN
54: Alistair Te Ariki Campbell / WHY DON'T YOU TALK TO ME?
55: James K. Baxter / A SMALL ODE ON MIXED FLATTING
56: David Mitchell / TH BALLAD OF ROSY CROCHET
57: Peter Olds / REVISITING V8 NOSTALGIA
58: Sam Hunt / MAINTRUNK COUNTRY ROADSONG
59: Ian Wedde / PATHWAY TO THE SEA
60: Florence E. Allan / WHAT NEXT?
61: Rore Hapipi / ANCESTORS
62: Murray Edmond / SHACK

63: Michael Jackson / MAKING IT OTHERWISE
64: Wystan Curnow / 'WHAT ARE KNOWN IN NEW ZEALAND . . . '
65: Apirana Taylor / SAD JOKE ON A MARAE
66: Allen Curnow / THE PARAKEETS AT KAREKARE
67: Lauris Edmond / THE NAMES
68: Keri Hulme / WHAKATU
69: Iain Sharp / A GAME FOR CHILDREN
70: Glennis Foster / NIGHT AND NOISES
71: John Newton / FERRET TRAP
72: Hugh Lauder / THE INVINCIBLE
73: Kim Eggleston / THE BACK ROAD BACK
74: Elizabeth Nannestad / BLACK DRESS
75: Amber McWilliams / OVER THE HARBOUR BRIDGE
76: Michael Morrissey / GOING OVER THE HARBOUR BRIDGE HAPPY POEM
77: Bob Orr / THELONIOUS MONK PIANO
78: Meg Campbell / VIOLA
79: Owen Marshall / THE DIVIDED WORLD
80: Roma Potiki / COMPULSORY CLASS VISITS
81: David Eggleton / POSTCARD
82: Michele Leggott / VANILLA RIM
83: Brian Turner / CHEVY
84: Geoff Cochrane / FOR BOB ORR, AGAIN
85: Elizabeth Smither / A CORTÈGE OF DAUGHTERS
86: Graham Lindsay / NORTHERN OAKS
87: Virginia Were / WE LISTEN FOR YOU ON THE RADIO
88: Jenny Bornholdt / MAKE SURE
89: Alan Riach / THE BLUES
90: Anne French / CABIN FEVER
91: Iain Lonie / PROPOSAL AT ALLANS BEACH
92: Bernadette Hall / BOWL
93: Michael Harlow / NO PROBLEM, BUT NOT EASY
94: Anne Kennedy / I WAS A FEMINIST IN THE EIGHTIES
95: Janet Charman / THE SMELL OF HER HAIR

96: Margaret Mahy / BUBBLE TROUBLE
97: Forbes Williams / FAST COLD
98: Andrew Johnston / HOW TO TALK
99: Damien Wilkins / MY FATHER'S STUTTER
100: C.K. Stead / AT THE GRAVE OF GOVERNOR HOBSON
101: Stephen Sinclair / THE HISTORIAN
102: Stephanie de Montalk / CONCRETE
103: John Clarke / WE DON'T KNOW HOW LUCKY WE ARE
104: Robert Sullivan / WAKA 99
105: David Geary / MARTON
106: Jo Randerson / WHY OUR WASHING MACHINE BROKE
107: Kapka Kassabova / SECURITY
108: Vivienne Plumb / THE TANK
109: Gregory O'Brien / ODE TO THE WAIHI BEACH DUMP
110: Emma Neale / LETTER TO FRIENDS FROM DALEY'S FLAT HUT: WALKING THE REES AND THE DART
111: Laura Ranger / TWO WORD POEM
112: Anna Jackson / FONTANELLO
113: Rhian Gallagher / THE QUIET PLACE
114: Chris Price / DOG'S BODY
115: Tusiata Avia / WILD DOGS UNDER MY SKIRT
116: Glenn Colquhoun / COMMUNION
117: Rachel Bush / THE STRONG MOTHERS
118: James Brown / I COME FROM PALMERSTON NORTH
119: Kate Camp / DOCUMENTARIES
120: Sonja Yelich / 1YA
121: Adrian Croucher / NOWHERE

notes

acknowledgements

index of authors

introduction

Choose one of the following, and discuss at length.
Either:
Poetry is going through a bad time. Everyone says so. No one buys the stuff. No one reads it. Or, if they read it, they read it reluctantly. Probably the internet will finish poetry off. It's incomprehensible, anyway. What happened to rhyme?
Or:
Poetry is enjoying a real renaissance. We have a national poetry day. And just consider the great human rites of passage. Go to a naming ceremony, a wedding, a funeral — you can be sure someone will read a poem. More and more, it's poetry that keeps us company on our way through life.

It's as well this isn't a multiple-choice question in an exam, as both points of view might be justified. My guess is that there are not all that many more committed readers of poetry early in the twenty-first century than when the first important anthology of New Zealand poetry in English, Alexander and Currie's *New Zealand Verse*, appeared in 1906. But poetry is now a far more familiar part of our landscape; it thrives beyond the library and the classroom. And the number of confident, adventurous poets currently writing is remarkable. A great variety of accomplished and astonishing new work has been produced in New Zealand in the dozen years since the publication of *100 New Zealand Poems*, the predecessor of this new volume.

That is a roundabout way of saying that the idea of adding 21 new poems to the 1993 anthology seemed easy enough at first. There were plenty to select from. But that is also why settling on the final 21 proved so hard. Which poets do you choose, given that so many are writing so well? And even harder, which *poems* do you choose, given that this is a collection where the conversations between poems are often as lively as the individual poems themselves?

Most anthologies strike a balance between variety and the need to show the quality of a few remarkable individual voices. In practice editors settle, quite properly, on twenty poems by Allen Curnow, say, or James K. Baxter, then tuck a range of other voices in around them. True to its subtitle as well as its title, *121 New Zealand Poems (by 121 New Zealand Poets)* opts for the widest possible embrace.

Of course, my final selection isn't inclusive: it represents my own preferences and prejudices, not all of which I consciously recognise. But alongside work by writers like Lauris Edmond and Denis Glover and Ian Wedde and Robin Hyde, I have tried to find room for song poems, prose poems and poems by children – and also for a few sports, like the wonderfully whimsical nineteenth-century love poem, 'The Married Antipodes'. I have emphasised poems where the writers point at the world around them. I have also sneaked in one or two *bad* poems, like Thomas Bracken's 'Not Understood', once New Zealand's best-known poem.

Another decision has heightened this sense of mixed voices and shifting perspectives. For the most part the poems are ordered not according to dates of first publication or authors' birthdates, but loosely according to the events they refer to. Thus Fiona Farrell's poem about a nineteenth-century serving girl, Charlotte O'Neil, makes more sense – or more interesting sense – next to John Barr of Craigielee's confident Scots cheer in 'There's Nae Place Like Otago Yet'. Conversely, Barr's poem looks shrewder, pawkier, less complacent, in the company of Farrell's. Where I have broken this rule, it has usually been for the sake of a particular encounter between two texts. Cilla McQueen's 'Living Here', for example, looked as if it might make its liveliest intervention quite near the beginning.

There is also a pragmatic reason for ordering the poems like this. It has enabled me to give the nineteenth-century some presence, without the obligation to include vast quantities of bad verse. I have avoided most of the weak Tennysonian warblings which once weighed upon the spirit of the land, although one or two passages in Anne Glenny Wilson's poem – 'I love this narrow sandy road / That idly gads o'er hill and vale' – will suggest what I have set aside.

That word 'vale' is one which William Hodgson (1826–94) vigorously defends in 'The Lay of the Weather-Bound', in the same breath decrying '*gully*, *creek*, and *scrub*' as words which simply make an ugly landscape uglier. In retrospect Hodgson is an interesting case. When his poems were posthumously published, their editor, Alfred Grace, was at pains to indicate where the author's loyalties lay: 'The poetry of the engine-room and f'oc'sle had no charm for William Hodgson; with him the classical models sufficed.' In fact, Hodgson's poems, like much early New Zealand versifying, could have done with much more of the engine-room and f'oc'sle, and with many more words like 'creek' and 'scrub' and 'gully'. The good-humoured fury of 'The Lay of the Weather-Bound' shows what might have been achieved if classical models had *not* sufficed.

Poems in anthologies always have their first life elsewhere. They are natives of another place. The passage from Lloyd Jones's award-winning rugby novel *The Book of Fame* (number 24) is only the most obvious example of a text that has a richer existence within a larger, earlier context. The same can be said for poems here by writers like Dinah Hawken, Anne Kennedy, Glenn Colquhoun and Kapka Kassabova. Even John Clarke's 'We Don't Know How Lucky We Are' has more texture when it is set among other songs and sketches involving the gumbooted Fred Dagg. Some poems, of course, do not survive transplantation from the place where they grew. That has been another factor governing my selection.

But then, every poem in this anthology has a prior relationship with other poems by its author. One almost invisible example: in Tusiata Avia's 'Wild Dogs Under My Skirt' there is a reference to 'Bingo'. Readers of the book from which the poem comes will know that it includes a warm, comic piece about a Samoan village dog called Bingo. In such a context, 'Wild Dogs Under My Skirt' has a slightly different edge to it than it has as poem number 115 in this selection.

Avia's poem has its own strong legs to stand on, however, and it gathers energy and resonance from the conversations it is able to have with other work in *121 New Zealand Poems*. Most obviously, it rubs shoulders with Chris Price's 'Dog's Body', but it can probably also hear distant barking from poems by Bruce Stronach and William Hart-Smith. I hope that my decision to leave authors' names off their poems (though of course the names are there on the contents pages and in the index of authors) gives the poems themselves freedom to move and to strike up a range of new relationships. For readers who want to track down original contexts or know more about particular writers, I have included further information in the endnotes, including the addresses of useful websites.

Alexander and Currie's 1906 anthology contained notes, too, along with an index of first lines which ended with the entry, 'Woe to the seekers of pleasure!' I hope that *121 New Zealand Poems* has plenty to offer the seekers of pleasure, that it will give those deep, ancient satisfactions for which poetry is famed: wisdom and delight. When *100 New Zealand Poems* was published, the last and 100th poem, written by seven-year-old Laura Ranger, was about the relationship between words and wisdom, and its last line allowed the book to end with the word *knowledge*. The final poem in *121 New Zealand Poems* ends with the words 'Now you know.' Well, maybe. Like the very best poems, Adrian Croucher's 'Nowhere' is about the surprise and satisfaction of stepping off the safe road. It leaves us in one of those places poetry likes to go to – where we can be lost and found at the very same time.

Bill Manhire
Wellington 2005

1

CHARM

I arrive where an unknown earth is under my feet,
I arrive where a new sky is above me,
I arrive at this land
                A resting place for me.
O spirit of the earth! the stranger humbly offers his heart
  As food for thee.

2

LIVING HERE

Well you have to remember this place
is just one big city with 3 million people with
a little flock of sheep each so we're all sort of
shepherds
          little human centres each within an outer
circle of sheep around us like a ring of
covered wagons   we all know we'll probably
be safe when the Indians finally come
down from the hills   (comfortable to live
in the Safest Place in the World)
                        sheep being
very thick & made of wool & leather
being a very effective shield as ancient
soldiers would agree.
               And you can also
sit on them of course & wear them & eat them
so after all we are lucky to have these
sheep in abundance   they might
have been hedgehogs – Then we'd all be
used to hedgehogs & clothed in prickles
rather than fluff
              & the little sheep would
come out sometimes at night under the moon
& we'd leave them saucers of milk
                        & feel sad
seeing them squashed on the road
Well anyway here we are with all this
cushioning in the biggest city in the world
its suburbs strung out in a long line

      & the civic centre at the bottom of
Cook Strait   some of them Hill Suburbs
& some Flat Suburbs & some more prosperous
than others
            some with a climate that embarrasses
them & a tendency to grow strange small fruit
some temperate & leafy   whose hot streets lull

So here we are again in the biggest
safest city in the world   all strung out
over 1500 miles one way   & a little bit
the other
          each in his woolly protection
so sometimes it's difficult to see out
the eyes   let alone call to each other
which is the reason for the loneliness some
of us feel
          and for our particular relations
with the landscape   that we trample
or stroke with our toes or eat or lick
tenderly or pull apart
            and love   like an
old familiar lover who fits us
curve to curve   and hate because it
knows us & knows our weakness
We're calling fiercely to each other
through the muffled spaces   grateful for
any wrist-brush
            cut of mind or touch of music,
lightning in the intimate weather of the soul.

3

A YOUNG WOMAN FORSAKEN BY HER LOVER

Look where the mist
Hangs over Pukehina.
There is the path
By which went my love.

Turn back again hither
That may be poured out
Tears from my eyes.

It was not I who first spoke of love.
You it was who made advances to me
When I was but a little thing.

Therefore was my heart made wild,
This is my farewell of love to thee.

4

GHOST SHIPS

If you look out at first light
you'll see on the harbour
the ships of our history
called back to life
by the sun's rekindling.
At dawn they discharge
guilty cargoes: ballast
spills in a gravelly bay,
musket cases, bayonets
wrapped in oilcloth,
are stacked on the shore.

There's a figure on the deck
dressed in serge, a high-
winged collar censures
his vision; he's taking the air
and whatever else
he can lay his hands on.

5

DAVID LOWSTON

My name is David Lowston
I did seal, I did seal.
My name is David Lowston, I did seal.
My men and I were lost,
Though our very lives 'twould cost,
We did seal, we did seal, we did seal.

'Twas in eighteen hundred and ten, we set sail, we set sail.
'Twas in eighteen hundred and ten, we set sail.
We were left, we gallant men,
Never more to sail again,
For to sail, for to sail, for to sail.

We were set down in Open Bay, were set down, were set down.
We were set down in Open Bay, were set down.
Upon the sixteenth day
Of Februar-aye-ay,
For to seal, for to seal, for to seal.

Our Captain, John Bedar, he set sail, he set sail.
Yes, for Port Jackson he set sail.
'I'll return, men, without fail!'
But she foundered in a gale,
And went down, and went down, and went down.

We cured ten thousand skins, for the fur, for the fur.
We cured ten thousand skins for the fur.
Brackish water, putrid seal,
We did all of us fall ill,
For to die, for to die, for to die.

Come all you sailor lads, who sail the sea, who sail the sea.
Come all you Jacks, who sail upon the sea.
Though the schooner *Governor Bligh*
Took on some who did not die,
Never seal, never seal, never seal!

6

THE MARRIED ANTIPODES

> To my Wife in London, by the Winds
> Overland, from the Antipodes

When last we parted in the glen,
We fondly hoped to meet again;
And, though 'twere even in the moon,
We vowed, in fact, and swore, in fine,
    Wherever plac'd, in earth or sky,
That, meeting, by the straightened line,
    Should yield to us the purest joy.
Yet, true it is, however strange,
In absence, oft, our notions change;
And, at this moment, should we meet,
    Each, straight descending through a hole,
Pois'd, as we are, with feet to feet,
    Our hearts apart, though sole to sole,
'Twould place us both in such a plight
As might not be exactly right.
For, think'st thou not, my dearest wife,
    On meeting in the central place,
Since we have ne'er been given to strife,
    That, in lieu of a sweet embrace,
'Twould grieve us much & make us sick
To greet each other with a kick!
    Believe me dear, tho' distant far,
    I am, as ever, yours, J.R.

7

THE NIGHT WATCH SONG OF THE 'CHARLOTTE JANE'

'Tis the first watch of the night, brothers,
    And the strong wind rides the deep;
And the cold stars shining bright, brothers,
    Their mystic courses keep.
Whilst our ship her path is cleaving
    The flashing waters through,
Here's a health to the land we are leaving,
    And the land we are going to!

First sadly bow the head, brothers,
    In silence o'er the wine,
To the memory of the dead, brothers,
    The fathers of our line –
Though their tombs may not receive us,
    Far o'er the ocean blue,
Their spirits ne'er shall leave us,
    In the land we are going to.

Whilst yet sad memories move us,
    A second cup we'll drain
To the manly hearts that love us,
    In our old homes o'er the main –
Fond arms that used to caress us,
    Sweet smiles from eyes of blue,
Lips which no more may bless us,
    In the land we are going to.

But away with sorrow now, brothers,
    Fill the winecup to the brim!
Here's to all who'll swear the vow, brothers,
    Of this our midnight hymn: —
That each man shall be a brother,
    Who has joined our gallant crew:
That we'll stand by one another
    In the land we are going to!

Fill again, before we part, brothers,
    Fill the deepest draught of all,
To the loved ones of our hearts, brothers,
    Who reward and share our toil —
From husbands and from brothers,
    All honour be their due, —
The noble maids and mothers
    Of the land we are going to! —

The wine is at an end, brothers;
    But ere we close our eyes,
Let a silent prayer ascend, brothers,
    For our gallant enterprise —
Should our toil be all unblest, brothers,
    Should ill winds of fortune blow,
May we find God's haven of rest, brothers,
    In the land we are going to.

THERE'S NAE PLACE LIKE OTAGO YET

There's nae place like Otago yet,
    There's nae wee beggar weans,
Or auld men shivering at our doors,
    To beg for scraps or banes.
We never see puir working folk
    Wi' bauchles on their feet,
Like perfect icicles wi' cauld,
    Gaun starving through the street.

We never hear o' breaking stanes
    A shilling by the yard;
Or poor folk roupit to the door
    To pay the needfu' laird;
Nae purse-proud, upstart, mushroom lord
    To scowl at honest toil,
Or break it down that he, the wretch,
    May feast on roast and boil.

My curse upon them, root and branch,
    A tyrant I abhor;
May despotism's iron foot
    Ne'er mark Otago's shore:
May wealth and labour hand in hand
    Work out our glorious plan,
But never let it be allowed
    That money makes the man.

9

CHARLOTTE O'NEIL'S SONG

You rang your bell and I answered.
I polished your parquet floor.
I scraped out your grate
and I washed your plate
and I scrubbed till my hands were raw.

You lay on a silken pillow.
I lay on an attic cot.
That's the way it should be, you said.
That's the poor girl's lot.
You dined at eight
and slept till late.
I emptied your chamber pot.
The rich man earns his castle, you said.
The poor deserve the gate.

But I'll never say 'sir'
or 'thank you ma'am'
and I'll never curtsy more.
You can bake your bread
and make your bed
and answer your own front door.

I've cleaned your plate
and I've cleaned your house
and I've cleaned the clothes you wore.
But now you're on your own, my dear.
I won't be there any more.
And I'll eat when I please
and I'll sleep where I please

and you can open your own front door.

10

**PIONEER WOMAN
WITH FERRETS**

Preserved in film,
As under glass,
Her waist nipped in,
Skirt and sleeves
To ankle, wrist,
Voluminous
In the wind,
Hat to protect
Her Victorian complexion,
Large in the tussock
She looms,
Startling as a moa.
Unfocused,
Her children
Fasten wire-netting
Round close-set warrens,
And savage grasses
That bristle in a beard
From the rabbit-bitten hills.
She is monumental
In the treeless landscape.
Nonchalantly she swings
In her left hand
A rabbit,
Bloodynose down,
In her right hand a club.

11

THE CHARGE AT PARIHAKA

Yet a league, yet a league
    Yet a league onward,
Straight to the Maori Pah
    Marched the Twelve Hundred.
'Forward the Volunteers!
Is there a man who fears?'
Over the ferny plain
    Marched the Twelve Hundred!

'Forward!' the Colonel said;
Was there a man dismayed?
No, for the heroes knew
    There was no danger.
Theirs not to reckon why,
Theirs not to bleed or die,
Theirs but to trample by:
    Each dauntless ranger.

Pressmen to right of them,
Pressmen to left of them,
Pressmen in front of them,
    Chuckled and wondered.
Dreading their country's eyes,
Long was the search and wise,
Vain, for the pressmen five
Had, by a slight device,
    Foiled the Twelve Hundred.

Gleamed all their muskets bare,
Fright'ning the children there,
Heroes to do and dare,
Charging a village, while
    Maoridom wondered.
Plunged in potato fields,
Honour to hunger yields.
Te Whiti and Tohu
Bearing not swords or shields,
Questioned nor wondered,
Calmly before them sat;
    Faced the Twelve Hundred.

Children to right of them,
Children to left of them,
Women in front of them,
    Saw them and wondered;
Stormed at with jeer and groan,
Foiled by the five alone,
Never was trumpet blown
    O'er such a deed of arms.
Back with their captives three
Taken so gallantly,
    Rode the Twelve Hundred.

When can their glory fade?
Oh! the wild charge they made,
    New Zealand wondered
Whether each doughty soul,
Paid for the pigs he stole:
    Noble Twelve Hundred!

12

PARIHAKA

The province has set up shrines
to its martyrs and heroes Te
Rangi Hiroa to the north
where his vikings landed von
Tempsky well to the south
at the scene of his last encounter
with the spirit of '48
the Richmond cottage with two
volumes of the *Evangelical
Magazine* (but Harry
Atkinson out with the militia
read Mill *On Liberty*
a year after publication)
colonial gothic St Mary's
with neat rows in the graveyard
soldiers sailors settlers
killed by the rebel natives
regimental hatchments
one for the Friendly Maoris
a 20th century second
thought in bright blond wood
to remember all who died
a patch on a war scarred face
no sign for Parihaka
a broken road a set
of ruinous foundations
charred remains of timber
a '38 Chevrolet
under the cloudy mountain.

THE DWELLINGS OF OUR DEAD

They lie unwatched, in waste and vacant places,
In sombre bush or wind-swept tussock spaces,
    Where seldom human tread
And never human trace is –
    The dwellings of our dead!

No insolence of stone is o'er them builded;
By mockery of monuments unshielded,
    Far on the unfenced plain
Forgotten graves have yielded
    Earth to free earth again.

Above their crypts no air with incense reeling,
No chant of choir or sob of organ pealing;
    But ever over them
The evening breezes kneeling
    Whisper a requiem.

For some the margeless plain where no one passes,
Save when at morning far in misty masses
    The drifting flock appears.
Lo, here the greener grasses
    Glint like a stain of tears!

For some the quiet bush, shade-strewn and saddened,
Whereo'er the herald tui, morning-gladdened,
    Lone on his chosen tree,
With his new rapture maddened,
    Shouts incoherently.

For some the gully, where in whispers tender,
The flax-blades mourn and murmur, and the slender
    White ranks of toi go,
With drooping plumes of splendour,
    In pageantry of woe.

For some the common trench where, not all fameless,
They fighting fell who thought to tame the tameless,
    And won their barren crown;
Where one grave holds them nameless –
    Brave white and braver brown.

But in their sleep, like troubled children turning,
A dream of mother-country in them burning,
    They whisper their despair,
And one vague, voiceless yearning
    Burdens the pausing air . . .

'Unchanging here the drab year onward presses;
No Spring comes trysting here with new-loosed tresses,
    And never may the years
Win Autumn's sweet caresses –
    Her leaves that fall like tears.

And we would lie 'neath old-remembered beeches,
Where we could hear the voice of him who preaches
    And the deep organ's call,
While close about us reaches
    The cool, grey lichened wall.'

But they are ours, and jealously we hold them;
Within our children's ranks we have enrolled them,

    And till all Time shall cease
Our brooding bush shall fold them
    In her broad-bosomed peace.

They came as lovers come, all else forsaking,
The bonds of home and kindred proudly breaking;
    They lie in splendour lone –
The nation of their making
    Their everlasting throne!

14

OUR CITIES FACE THE SEA

Jack came from Cornwall, and Pat from Donegal
'Arry came from London, the first place of all,
Sandy came from Aberdeen, and Tom's native-born,
But they're all mates together in the lands of the morn.
    Pulling, pulling on the one rope together,
    Bringing up the future with a golden tether,
Cousin Jack and Cockney, Irishman and Scot,
And the native is a brother to the whole blooming lot.

He worked at Gabriel's gully, he was there at the Dunstan rush,
He was first when the reefing opened and the batteries started to crush;
He was favourite ever with fortune, and whatever he touched would pay,
And his life was a song with the chorus, 'I'm going home some day.'
But he made his home on the hillside where the city faces the sea,
And he saw the houses rising and the children on his knee,
And he toiled, and laughed, and was happy, as the years went rolling by;
For we take our homeland with us, however we change our sky.

He thought of a far-off village, and a steeple grey with years,
The cottages white in the sunshine, and a parting day of tears;
He saw the gardens blooming with lavender around the beds,
And the doors that were bowered with roses that nodded over their heads;
He heard the thrushes singing, and the sparrows chirping at morn;
He saw the joy of the hay-time, and the poppies that starred the corn;
But up on the bush-covered hill-side the years went laughing by;
For we take our homeland with us, however we change our sky.

He left the windy city for the home beyond the sea, –
He would spend his age in the village beneath the old roof-tree;

He would hear again the ringing of the mellow Sunday bell,
And the folk would gather round him for the tales he had to tell,
The glamour of days long faded he would gather again anew;
He would see the happy meadows and the daisies washed in dew –
He went, and he saw, and he wearied, and ever his thoughts would fly
To another and dearer homeland under another sky.

He had learned the charm of the mountains, the breath of the tussocks he knew;
He had lived in a land of sunshine, under skies of cloudless blue;
And the charm of the old had faded, as the charm of the new had grown,
Till he hailed the windy islands with their flax and fern as his own,
Till he thought with a tender longing of lake, and mountain, and plain,
And the digger's camp in the gully, with its toil and its laughter again.
The old land could not hold him, its ways were sere and dry;
For we take our homeland with us in youth when we change our sky.

Our cities look to the ocean, the homeland is far away;
The ships come sailing, sailing, and anchor in the bay;
Oh, tender the ties that bind us to the land our fathers knew,
And rich the storied record of a people strong and true;
Our thoughts will linger fondly in the North-land far away,
But our own land, our homeland is where we live to-day.
For together in toil and laughter the years go rolling by,
And we take our homeland with us, however we change our sky.

Jack came from Cornwall, and Pat from Donegal
'Arry came from London, the first place of all,
Sandy came from Aberdeen, and Tom's native-born,
But they're all mates together in the lands of the morn.
    Pulling, pulling on the one rope together,
    Bringing up the future with a golden tether.
Cousin Jack and Cockney, Irishman and Scot,
And the native is a brother to the whole blooming lot.

    Pulling, pulling on the one rope strong
        Bringing up the future with a shout and a song,
But the tides rise and fall, and the steamers come to call,
And the cities face the sea, and the winds are blowing free,
And out across the ocean is our home after all.

15

THE TUG OF WAR

Is a scene that rises in her mind. A long line of men, say 100,
facing north, holding a long rope. A long line of women, say 110,
facing south, facing the men, holding the same long rope.
They are all dressed in late 19th century clothes, standing ready
on the shore-line of a long New Zealand beach. A long line
of surf is breaking.

                    The rope is clearly visible in the gap
where the first man faces the first woman. Here the starter also
stands. He is shouting into the megaphone:
'Take the strain – get ready – go!' So the tug
of war begins. Equal weight and equal strength on each
side. Centuries of struggle are rising
in the blood of each man and each woman and at the exact
moment that they judge the men to be at the height
of their physical and mental power, the women
let the rope go.

    They love to let go and they love to get going:
    they get themselves going and they let themselves go.
    They let love go and they get love going:
    they get others going and they let others go.
    They let life go and they get life going,
    they live to give love and they love to let live.

NOT UNDERSTOOD

Not understood, we move along asunder;
    Our paths grow wider as the seasons creep
Along the years; we marvel and we wonder
    Why life is life, and then we fall asleep
        Not understood.

Not understood, we gather false impressions
    And hug them closer as the years go by;
Till virtues often seem to us transgressions;
    And thus men rise and fall, and live and die
        Not understood.

Not understood! Poor souls with stunted vision
    Oft measure giants with their narrow gauge;
The poisoned shafts of falsehood and derision
    Are oft impelled 'gainst those who mould the age,
        Not understood.

Not understood! The secret springs of action
    Which lie beneath the surface and the show,
Are disregarded; with self-satisfaction
    We judge our neighbours, and they often go
        Not understood.

Not understood! How trifles often change us!
    The thoughtless sentence and the fancied slight
Destroy long years of friendship, and estrange us,
    And on our souls there falls a freezing blight;
        Not understood.

Not understood! How many breasts are aching
    For lack of sympathy! Ah! day by day
How many cheerless, lonely hearts are breaking!
    How many noble spirits pass away,
        Not understood.

O God! that men would see a little clearer,
    Or judge less harshly where they cannot see!
O God! that men would draw a little nearer
    To one another, – they'd be nearer Thee,
        Not understood.

17

BEGINNINGS

Guthrie-Smith in New Zealand 1885

Who am I? What am I doing here
alone with 3000 sheep? I'm
turning their bones into grass. Later
I'll turn grass back into sheep.
I buy only the old and the lame.
They eat anything – bush, bracken, gorse.
Dead, they melt into one green fleece.

Who am I? I know the Lord's my shepherd
as I am theirs – but this
is the 19th century; Darwin
is God's First Mate. I must keep
my own log, full of facts if not love.
I own 10,000 acres and one dark lake.
On the seventh day those jaws don't stop.

Who am I? I am the one sheep
that must not get lost. So
I name names – rocks, flowers, fish:
knowing this place I learn to know myself.
I survive. The land becomes
my meat and tallow. I light my own lamps.
I hold back the dark with the blood of my lambs.

18

A SPRING AFTERNOON
IN NEW ZEALAND

We rode in the shadowy place of pines,
    The wind went whispering here and there
    Like whispers in a house of prayer.
The sunshine stole in narrow lines,
    And sweet was the resinous atmosphere,
    The shrill cicada, far and near,
Piped on his high exultant third.
    Summer! Summer! he seems to say –
Summer! He knows no other word,
    But trills on it the live-long day;
The little hawker of the green,
Who calls his wares through all the solemn forest scene.

A shadowy land of deep repose!
Here when the loud nor'wester blows,
How sweet, to soothe a trivial care,
The pine-trees' ever-murmured prayer!
To shake the scented powder down
    From stooping boughs that bar the way,
And see the vistas, golden brown,
    Touch the blue heaven far away.
But on and upward still we ride
    Whither the furze, an outlaw bold,
Scatters along the bare hillside
Handfuls of free, uncounted gold,
And breaths of nutty, wild perfume,
Salute us from the flowering broom.

I love this narrow, sandy road,
    That idly gads o'er hill and vale,
Twisting where once a rivulet flowed,
    With as many turns as a gossip's tale.
I love this shaky, creaking bridge,
And the willow leaning from the ridge,
    Shaped like some green fountain playing,
And the twinkling windows of the farm,
Just where the woodland throws an arm
    To hear what the merry stream is saying.

Stop the horses for a moment, high upon the breezy stair,
Looking over plain and upland, and the depth of summer air,
Watch the cloud and shadow sailing o'er the forest's sombre breast;
Misty capes and snow-cliffs glimmer on the ranges to the west.
Hear the distant thunder rolling; surely 'tis the making tide,
Swinging all the blue Pacific on the harbour's iron side. . . .
Now the day grows grey and chill, but see on yonder wooded fold,
Between the clouds a ray of sunshine slips, and writes a word in gold.

19

THE LAY OF THE WEATHER-BOUND

(Written at Sludgeville, Pactolus Country.)

Gods! how I loathe the land between
    These mountains and the sea,
Its wealth of all things vile and mean
    Is horrible to me.
No tuft of grass dare rear its head
    Above the sodden soil,
With rush and slimy moss o'erspread
    To mock the yeoman's toil.
In yonder woods there is no bird,
    In yonder brakes no flower,
Amid whose sunless depths is heard
    Naught but the ceaseless shower
From weeping skies — well may they weep
    To look on such a scene!
Whereat the sun just deigns to peep,
    Six weeks each glimpse between.
Vale, brook, and grove, to poet dear,
    Here changing name and dress,
As *gully*, *creek*, and *scrub* appear,
    In conscious ugliness.
A sight like this met Noah's eyes,
    When from his stranded Ark
He watched the dripping hill-tops rise
    Above high-water mark.
Dame Nature, when her task was done,
    That nothing might be lost,
Picked up the refuse scraps in fun,
    And fashioned the West Coast.

20

SONG OF THE GUMFIELD

In the slighted, blighted North where the giant kauris grow,
And the earth is bare and barren where the bush-bee used to hum,
And the luck we've followed's failing and our friends are out of hailing,
And it's getting narrow sailing by the rocks of Kingdom Come,
There's a way of fighting woe, squaring store-bills as you go,
In the trade of digging gum.

And the new chum and the scum
And the scouring of the slum,
And the lawyer and the doctor, and the deaf and halt and dumb,
And the parson and the sailor, and the welsher and the whaler,
When the world is looking glum,
Just to keep from Kingdom Come,
Take to digging kauri gum.

In the scrubby, grubby North when the giddy sun is set,
And the idiot-owl-cicada stops the whirring of his drum;
And the night is growing thicker and the bottled candles flicker,
And the damned mosquitoes bicker in a diabolic hum,
There's a way of ending fret and of pulling down a debt
In the task of scraping gum.

And the new chum and the scum
And the scouring of the slum,
And the lawyer and the doctor, and the deaf and halt and dumb,
And the parson and the sailor, and the welsher and the whaler,
When the world is looking glum,
Just to keep from Kingdom Come,
Take to scraping kauri gum.

In the sloppy, floppy North through the dismal winter rain,
When the man is merely muscle and the mind is nearly numb,
When the old, old pains rheumatic fill the bones from base to attic
And a sound of words erratic sets the pannikins a-thrum,
There's a way of killing Cain and an antidote to pain
In the task of hooking gum.

And the new chum and the scum
And the scouring of the slum,
And the lawyer and the doctor, and the deaf and halt and dumb,
And the parson and the sailor, and the welsher and the whaler,
When the world is looking glum,
Just to keep from Kingdom Come,
Take to hooking kauri gum.

And the man of law has gambled through another man's estate,
And the doctor's special weakness at the present time is rum,
And the parson loves the clocking on a pretty maiden's stocking,
And his stories (mostly shocking) scare the neophyte new chum.
By the smouldering ti-tree fire, when the wind is howling higher,
They are cracking jokes that blister the Recording Angel's slate,
And the matters that they mention are too primitive to state
At the scraping of the gum.

But the new chum and the scum
And the scouring of the slum,
And the lawyer and the doctor, and the deaf and halt and dumb,
And the parson and the sailor, and the welsher and the whaler,
When the Day of Judgement's come
Oh, won't they be looking glum!
As the mighty trumpets thunder and the harps go tinkle-tum,
And they've finished with the digging and they've scraped the final crumb,
And the bottom's gone for ever from the trade of kauri gum.

THE OLD PLACE

So the last day's come at last, the close of my fifteen year —
The end of the hope, an' the struggles, an' messes I've put in here.
All of the shearings over, the final mustering done, —
Eleven hundred an' fifty for the incoming man, near on.
Over five thousand I drove 'em, mob by mob, down the coast;
Eleven-fifty in fifteen year . . . it isn't much of a boast.

Oh, it's a bad old place! Blown out o' your bed half the nights,
And in summer the grass burnt shiny an' bare as your hand, on the heights:
The creek dried up by November, and in May a thundering roar
That carries down toll o' your stock to salt 'em whole on the shore.
Clear'd I have, and I've clear'd an' clear'd, yet everywhere, slap in your face,
Briar, tauhinu, an' ruin! — God! it's a brute of a place.
. . . An' the house got burnt which I built, myself, with all that worry and pride;
Where the Missus was always homesick, and where she took fever, and died.

Yes, well! I'm leaving the place. Apples look red on that bough.
I set the slips with my own hand. Well — they're the other man's now.
The breezy bluff: an' the clover that smells so over the land,
Drowning the reek o' the rubbish, that plucks the profit out o' your hand:

That bit o' Bush paddock I fall'd myself, an' watched, each year, come clean
(Don't it look fresh in the tawny? A scrap of Old-Country green):
This air, all healthy with sun an' salt, an' bright with purity:
An' the glossy karakas there, twinkling to the big blue twinkling sea:

Ay, the broad blue sea beyond, an' the gem-clear cove below,
Where the boat I'll never handle again, sits rocking to and fro:
There's the last look to it all! an' now for the last upon
This room, where Hetty was born, an' my Mary died, an' John . . .

Well, I'm leaving the poor old place, and it cuts as keen as a knife;
The place that's broken my heart – the place where I've lived my life.

22

THE WINDY HILLS O' WELLINGTON

The windy hills o' Wellington were black and cold that night,
The rain came down at times, enough to drown the 'lectric light;
An' like a hymn of hate and want from black misfortune's choirs
I heard the cruel, spiteful wind go snarling thro' the wires.
An' from the winches by the wharf a rattle and a clank,
While sitting by a Sydney chum who's drawn New Zealand blank!

He'd sent for me, in all the land the only chum he knew,
His health and hope and cash were gone – and he was going too,
His frame was shrunk, his face was drawn, his eyes were blear'd and dim,
For drink and poverty and want had done their work for him;
And when I came, he turned to me, his features pale and lank –
I'm glad you came, old chum,' he said, *'I've drawn New Zealand blank!'*

' "New leaf, new land", my motto was – I did my very best.
'Twas want of work that threw me back – an' liquor did the rest.
But nothing matters now, old man – it never did, no doubt
(Excuse a little nonsense when a fellow's peggin' out).
I'd live and fight if I had hope or money at the bank.
I've lived too long in '94, I've drawn New Zealand blank!'

I looked out through the window as the rain came pelting down;
The great black hills they seemed to close and loom above the town.
And in a strained and tired voice, that filled my heart with pain,
He said, 'Old man, I'd like to stroll down George Street once again.
I had myself to "battle" for; I've got myself to thank.
Perhaps it ain't New Zealand's fault that I've drawn New Zealand blank.'

The breezy hills o' Wellington are fair as they can be.
I stand and watch a Sydney boat go sailing out to sea.
And while the sun is setting low on blue and brown and green,
I think of cruel things that are, and things that might have been,
And while the same old sun goes down in clouds a golden bank,
I sadly think of my old chum who drew New Zealand blank.

No headstone marks his resting-place – no autumn grasses wave –
And not a sign of loving hands is seen above his grave;
For he recover'd from the spree – the doctors pulled him through;
His health came back and his luck turned (and so did my luck, too) –
He now has houses, land and shares, and thousands in the bank;
He doesn't know me now, because – I've drawn New Zealand blank.

THE FIRST TRIBUTE

FOR MATTHEW MCKINNEY

Leaning on a prop in a Queen Street studio
with the easy, smiling charm of a chap
accustomed to saloon bars and piano lids,

natty in his volunteer uniform,
cap cocked like a dandy,
a slight swagger in his style,

as though he had just scored long odds
on a sure thing, stands the ancestor
whose grace and dash my own face mocks.

One can almost catch a whiff
of the Macassar and the brandy,
hear the fastidious snip of scissor at moustache

and read the intimacy in the eye –
the knock-out at the tables
and the lady-killer,

so soon to die in a matter of honour.
How the stench of the muck called food
must have stuck in those grand, discerning nostrils.

An Antipodean, back-blocks soldier-boy
posing as the Irish gent. The gallant contradictions
of irrational suicide.

Yet honour, when it grabs a man and twists,
grants no quick release – it will squeeze
down through the decades till at last

the truth comes out – and as he gazes
from his failed anonymity and says into the lens:
I won't be coming back – I'll see to that,

not flinching at the explosion of magnesium
while the photographer commands: *Stand still.
Don't move an inch. Let's see the whites of your eyes,*

and, upright, chivalrous and doomed,
pictures himself presented to the flare of guns
and the immaculate despatch of a Boer bullet,

one virtuous flash, a mortal sin outwitted
and a world put to right, time calls him back
and prompts: *It wasn't at all like that.*

*It was just heat and more heat –
and always the black thunderstorm of the flies –
till your meat melted from your bones.*

The heroic and romantic death he sought
sluiced through his bowels.
The Imperial Design preserved a few years more,

for what? For further sacrifice?
And was the woman worth it?
As it turned out the principle at stake

was stainless in its ignorance.
It all concerned a chaste deformity, a blockage,
which could have been adjusted by simple surgery.

No guilt. No one to blame.
But there he went to self-destruction,
with the band playing and my grandfather in tears.

Our first, colonial tribute of prime soldiery.
A blundering, Hawkes Bay Fenian,
dying for the Queen.

A fable in a battledress
and now a family memory. An obscure story,
complete with faded ikon

and a campaign-medal, like a relic, on a scrap
of ribbon not long enough to tie a single curl
of the wife whose shame he would conceal —

the shy conspirator in his death
who packed her widow's bags then went,
leaving no forwarding address.

24

HOW WE THINK

Our industry was football and experiments with space.

What we knew
what we understood
had no beautiful language at its service
lacked for artists and sculptors
what we knew was intimate
as instinct or memory

Our knowledge hinged on the word 'like'.

We could say that, that tree there
is like
our beech
or that woman's eye
caught between secrecy
and full disclosure
is sloped
like
a fig

Or we could say 'like'
when we needed time to think
what it was exactly
that needed explanation

'Like' was the hinge
on which unknowingness swung into light
we could say 'like'
when we meant 'imagine this'

For example, Billy Stead describing our 'pleasure principle' to a
newspaperman –

to glide outside a man is
like
pushing on a door
and coming through
to a larger world
      a glorious feeling
      like
      science
      sweet
      immaculate
      truth

Space was our medium
our play stuff
we championed the long view
the vista
the English settled for the courtyard

THE CITY FROM THE HILLS

There lies our city folded in the mist,
Like a great meadow in an early morn
Flinging her spears of grass up through white films,
Each with its thousand thousand-tinted globes.

Above us such an air as poets dream,
The clean and vast wing-winnowed clime of Heaven.

Each of her streets is closed with shining Alps,
Like Heaven at the end of long plain lives.

ANZAC SNAP

'The soldier is F. Come (NZ), to be killed soon after on the crest of Chunuk Bayir.'

Churchill sat in a smoky chair
and watched the London rain:
We'll chase the Turks to Hell, he said,
and chase them back again.

The Beautiful Battalions sailed
under a seething sky:
they landed at Gallipoli
to do his work and die.

*We'll be in Consty-nobble soon
and drinking pink champagne,
and then we'll get our medals, boys,
and sail back home again.*

But X was full of dying men
and Y was full of dead,
and Heaven, boys, was full of shells
that whistled overhead.

*O Johnny Turk keeps shooting, boys,
so keep your heads down low:
we'll be in Consty-nobble soon,
cos Churchill tells us so.*

I just stood up to see the sea.
It's quiet, boys, I said,
and something whistled through the sky
and hit me in the head.

The farm is still at Paterau,
the sheep graze by the sea,
and men ride up and down the bush
who've never heard of me.

O History is made by men
with nothing else to do.
They watch the rain, and have ideas
to try on me and you.

But glory isn't Names and Noise,
it isn't Arms and Men:
it's living out the little life
I'll never live again.

TO L.H.B.

Last night for the first time since you were dead
I walked with you, my brother, in a dream.
We were at home again beside the stream
Fringed with tall berry bushes, white and red.
'Don't touch them: they are poisonous,' I said.
But your hand hovered, and I saw a beam
Of strange, bright laughter flying round your head,
And as you stooped I saw the berries gleam.
'Don't you remember? We called them Dead Man's Bread!'
I woke and heard the wind moan and the roar
Of the dark water tumbling on the shore.
Where — where is the path of my dream for my eager feet?
By the remembered stream my brother stands
Waiting for me with berries in his hands . . .
'These are my body. Sister, take and eat.'

28

RESPONSE

When you wrote your letter it was April,
And you were glad that it was spring weather,
And that the sun shone out in turn with showers of rain.

I write in waning May and it is autumn,
And I am glad that my chrysanthemums
Are tied up fast to strong posts,
So that the south winds cannot beat them down.
I am glad that they are tawny coloured,
And fiery in the low west evening light.
And I am glad that one bush warbler
Still sings in the honey-scented wattle . . .

But oh, we have remembering hearts,
And we say 'How green it was in such and such an April,'
And 'Such and such an autumn was very golden,'
And 'Everything is for a very short time.'

29

OLD MEMORIES OF EARTH

I think I have no other home than this
    I have forgotten much remember much
    but I have never any memories such
    as these make out they have of lands of bliss.

Perhaps they have done, will again do what
    they say they have, drunk as gods on godly drink,
    but I have not communed with gods I think
    and even though I live past death shall not.

I rather am for ever bondaged fast
    to earth and have been: so much untaught I know.
    Slow like great ships often I have seen go
    ten priests ten each time round a grave long past

And I recall I think I can recall
    back even past the time I started school
    or went a-crusoeing in the corner pool
    that I was present at a city's fall

And I am positive that yesterday
    walking past One Tree Hill and quite alone
    to me there came a fellow I have known
    in some old times, but when I cannot say:

Though we must have been great friends, I and he,
    otherwise I should not remember him
    for everything of the old life seems dim
    as last year's deeds recalled by friends to me.

THE BUSHFELLER

Lord, mind your trees to-day!
My man is out there clearing.
God send the chips fly safe.
My heart is always fearing.

And let the axehead hold!
My dreams are all of felling.
He earns our bread far back.
And then there is no telling.

If he came home at nights,
We'd know, but it is only –
We might not even hear –
A man could lie there lonely.

God, let the trunks fall clear,
He did not choose his calling;
He's young and full of life –
A tree is heavy, falling.

31

TREES

Trees, they're funny things –
    They hurt somehow;
I've seen the whole sky caught
    In one black bough.

Pines I've loved best.
    You hear the sea,
All swelling soft and hoarse
    In just one tree.

They stand all black and tall,
    With stars between
Their strong dark boughs some nights.
    I know. I've seen.

I've watched trees drag and droop;
    Seems they weren't meant
For towns – all crying 'gainst
    The sky, and bent.

That hurt a bit, but pines –
    They stir me deep,
That soft, lost roar of theirs;
    They never sleep.

They hurt somehow, do trees.
    I've loved them all,
But pines, they twist my heart
    With their wild call.

THE MAGPIES

When Tom and Elizabeth took the farm
    The bracken made their bed,
And *Quardle oodle ardle wardle doodle*
    The magpies said.

Tom's hand was strong to the plough
    Elizabeth's lips were red,
And *Quardle oodle ardle wardle doodle*
    The magpies said.

Year in year out they worked
    While the pines grew overhead,
And *Quardle oodle ardle wardle doodle*
    The magpies said.

But all the beautiful crops soon went
    To the mortgage-man instead,
And *Quardle oodle ardle wardle doodle*
    The magpies said.

Elizabeth is dead now (it's years ago)
    Old Tom went light in the head;
And *Quardle oodle ardle wardle doodle*
    The magpies said.

The farm's still there. Mortgage corporations
    Couldn't give it away.
And *Quardle oodle ardle wardle doodle*
    The magpies say.

33

WALKING ON MY FEET

hitched up my bundle
went down the street
long way to go
walking on my feet

went past Charley's
didn't turn in
broke to the wide
had a good spin

toting my gunny
hit the south road
long way to go
got a heavy load

tired already
walking on my feet
dust in my mouth
and damn this heat

bloke just passed
had a spare seat
left me behind
walking on my feet

all my life
always on the go
keep on doing
the old heel and toe

put one in front
then put the other
same old way
I learnt from my mother

blister on my heel
don't know when I'll eat
same old business
walking on my feet

I know where I'm going
walking on my feet
reckon when I get there
I'll be dead beat

won't get a woman
won't find gold
pockets will be empty
bed will be cold

never will be worried
never want a snack
don't worry lady
I won't be back

I know where I'm going
where I'll lie down
nice quiet place
long way from town

long way to go
I'll sleep all alone
fingers round the earth
earth round the bone

living rent free
on easy street
never any more
go walking on my feet

34

JOHNNY COME DANCING

to Long John Montgomery

1
On Douglas Bridge
On Douglas Bridge
They were dancing! Dancing!
And he seventeen swinging home
Through the twilight
A day's work done
And not a care in his head
Stopping in wonder
What dancing! Dancing!
Their black curls bouncing
And their red shoes flashing
Five little girls – dancing! Dancing!
With their dark eyes gleaming
And their green dresses shining
Saying – Dance Johnny! Dance!
And we'll give you a shilling!
And he danced and he danced
And he danced till the dawning
Then they were gone
With the grey of the morning
And Johnny limped home
Clutching a shilling
And his mother cried out
And covered her head
Oh! Johnny my darling
You were not in your bed

And the fairies were out
On Douglas Bridge
Did you dance with them Johnny?
Did they give you a penny?
When he showed her the shilling
She kissed him goodbye
Then she wrapped him a loaf
And a coat for the weather
And that was the last
They were ever together.

2
He wept and he cursed
And he called to his mother
But the five little girls
Dragged him down to the river
Then he begged and he pleaded
That they take back their shilling
But they shook their dark heads
– It's no good your crying
You danced for our shilling
Now you'll dance till you're dying
You'll dance down the road
And you'll dance to the sea
And you'll dance till you reach
The last country
But it won't all be sorrow
Though you'll always be lonely
And you'll weep when you hear
The wild north wind calling
Then they jumped in the river
And when he looked over
There was only a swirl
And the sound of their laughter.

3
So he walked to Lough Foyle
And he met a sea captain
One man short
To sail for New Zealand
Where's that? asked Johnny
Is it far far away?
It's further than that
And we sail in the morning
I'll come then said Johnny
There's nothing to stop me
If I turn back now
The wee folk will get me
And I'll drown in the river
Below Douglas Bridge
And I'll always be cold
And I'll never be resting
For the five little girls
Will be dancing and leaping
And my dear dear mother
By the bridge there weeping.

4
So he sailed for New Zealand
On the outgoing tide
And it wasn't all pain
And it wasn't all grieving
Just so long
As he kept on dancing
And the new land was almost
As green as Ireland
And he married a girl
With her black hair waving

And she led him a dance
And she sneered at his pining
For a two-roomed cottage
With a rammed earth floor
And nothing to keep
The wolf from the door
And she scoffed at his stories
Of little girls dancing
With their black curls bouncing
And their red shoes flashing
But she stopped when she saw
His quick feet flying
For where had she ever
Seen such dancing! Dancing!
With his long legs weaving
And his blue eyes sparkling.

5
So he danced through the years
Through the love and the hating
Through the birth of his children
And her final betrayal
And he danced to his death
One mild spring evening
And he called out her name
As he fell to the floor
And the five little girls
Came through the door
And as he lay dying
He saw so clearly
They all had her face
And her black hair waving
With their dark eyes gleaming

And their green dresses shining
And the very last thing
That he ever saw
Was her dancing . . . dancing . . .
. . . dancing

THE ISLANDS

Always, in these islands, meeting and parting
Shake us, making tremulous the salt-rimmed air;
Divided and perplexed the sea is waiting,
Birds and fishes visit us and disappear.

The future and the past stand at our doors,
Beggars who for one look of trust will open
Worlds that can answer our unknown desires,
Entering us like rain and sun to ripen.

Remindingly beside the quays, the white
Ships lie smoking; and from their haunted bay
The godwits vanish towards another summer.
Everywhere in light and calm the murmuring
Shadow of departure; distance looks our way;
And none knows where he will lie down at night.

SHE WAS MY LOVE
WHO COULD DELIVER

She was my love who could deliver
From paws of pain and melancholy,
And light the lamps that burn forever,
And cleanse a page of screeds of folly,
And with a motion of her hand
Could reap a harvest on my land.

And she could melt an iron mood,
And lashing cords with love were softer,
And she could bring my course to good,
Could renovate with raining laughter,
And eye and heart her beauty brace
When death approached with peering face.

Against a secret shaft of malice
Piercing my solitary isle
She would defend with flying solace,
And visitations of her smile,
And from the spirit's blank occasions,
And from the craft of days and seasons
She was my love who could deliver.

from THE BEACHES

Close under here, I watched two lovers once,
Which should have been a sin, from what you say:
I'd come to look for prawns, small pale-green ghosts,
Sea-coloured bodies tickling round the pool.
But tide was out then; so I strolled away
And climbed the dunes, to lie here warm, face down,
Watching the swimmers by the jetty-posts
And wrinkling like the bright blue wrinkling bay.
It wasn't long before they came; a fool
Could see they had to kiss; but your pet dunce
Didn't quite know men count on more than that;
And so just lay, patterning sand.
                                        And they
Were pale thin people, not often clear of town;
Elastic snapped, when he jerked off her hat:
I heard her arguing, 'Dick, my frock!' But he
Thought she was bread.
                       I wished her legs were brown,
And mostly, then, stared at the dawdling sea,
Hoping Perry would row me some day in his boat.

Not all the time; and when they'd gone, I went
Down to the hollow place where they had been,
Trickling bed through fingers. But I never meant
To tell the rest, or you, what I had seen:
Though that night, when I came in late for tea,
I hoped you'd see the sandgrains on my coat.

TIME

Upon the benchy hillside
Where hoggets love to lie,
With noses pointed to the wind
And half-closed eye,
I walked alone on Sundays,
And wished my love was nigh.
For oh! the hours went slower
Than the moon goes in the sky.

Upon the benchy hillside
Raked with wind and sun,
Where the gray hawk hovers
And little rabbits run,
My love and I did linger
A few short hours;
But time slipped through our fingers,
As the wind slips through the flowers!

39

A NOTE ON THE RUSSIAN WAR

The sunflowers got us, the black seeds stuck in our hair, my mother went about saying in a high voice like the wind sunflowers kiddies, ah sunflowers.

We lived on the Steppes, my mother and the rest of my family and I, but mostly my Mother because she was bigger than the rest. She stood outside in the sun. She held a sunflower in her hand. It was the biggest blackest sunflower in Russia, and my mother said over and over again ah sunflowers.

I shall never forget being in Russia. We wore big high boots in the winter, and in the summer we went barefoot and wriggled our toes in the mud whenever it rained, and when there was snow on the ground we went outside under the trees to sing a Russian song, it went like this, I'm singing it to myself so you can't hear, tra-tra-tra, something about sunflowers and a tall sky and the war rolling through the grass, tra-tra-tra, it was a very nice song that we sang.

In space and time.

There are no lands outside, they are fenced inside us, a fence of being and we are the world my Mother told us we are Russian because we have this sunflower in our garden.

It grew in those days near the cow-byre and the potato patch. It was a little plant with a few little black seeds sometimes, and a scraggy flower with a black heart, like a big daisy only yellow and black, but it was too tall for us to see properly, the daisies were nearer our size.

All day on the lawn we made daisy chains and buttercup chains, sticking our teeth through the bitter stems.

All day on the lawn, don't you remember the smell of them, the new white daisies, you stuff your face amongst them and you put the buttercups under your chin to see if you love butter, and you do love butter anyway so what's the use, but the yellow shadow is Real Proof, 0 you love early, sitting amongst the wet painted buttercups.

And then out of the spring and summer days the War came. An ordinary war like the Hundred Years or the Wars of the Roses or the Great War where my

Father went and sang 'Tipperary'. All of the soldiers on my Father's side sang 'Tipperary', it was to show they were getting somewhere, and the louder they sang it the more sure they felt about getting there.

And the louder they sang it the more scared they felt inside.

Well in the Russian War we didn't sing 'Tipperary' or 'Pack Up Your Troubles' or 'There's A Long Long Trail A-Winding'.

We had sunflowers by the fence near where the fat white cow got milked. We had big high boots in winter.

We were just Russian children on the Steppes, singing tra-tra-tra, quietly with our Mother and Father, but war comes whatever you sing.

LAST RUN

He'd fallen over a cliff
And he'd broken his leg.
Just a mustering dog.
And he looked at me, there on the hill,
Showing no hurt, as if he'd taken no ill,
And his ears, and his tail,
And his dark eyes too,
Said plainly,
'Well, Boss, what do we do?
Any more sheep to head?
Give me a run.'
But he'd never head sheep any more.

His day was done.
He thought it was fun
When I lifted the gun.

SUBJECT MATTER

No, I think a footsore sheep dog
obeying the weary whistle with a limp
or a close-up of gorse
lit with headlamps
leaning out all dusty at night
toward a brother thorn across the road;
or a stand of pine
lopped for firewood; yes, and a
solitary cabbage-tree with its head blown off
a scraggy ruff of dead leaves
rattling at its neck. Not
these great chunks of landscape, Mount
Cook's fourteen guineas, rain on the
hills, south of this
and north of that. Please
paint me a pub winder
with the din behind it.

THE WIFE SPEAKS

Being a woman, I am
not more than man nor less
but answer imperatives
of shape and growth. The bone
attests the girl with dolls,
grown up to know the moon
unwind her tides to chafe
the heart. A house designs
my day an artifact
of care to set the hands
of clocks, and hours are round
with asking eyes. Night puts
an ear on silence where
a child may cry. I close
my books and know events
are people, and all roads
everywhere walk home
women and men, to take
history under their roofs.
I see Icarus fall
out of the sky, beside
my door, not beautiful,
envy of angels, but feathered
for a bloody death.

BEFORE THE FALL

After the bath with ragged towels
my Dad
would dry us very carefully:
six little wriggly girls,
each with foamy pigtails,
two rainy legs,
the invisible back we couldn't reach,
a small wet heart,
and toes, ten each.

He dried us all
the way he gave the parish
Morning Prayer:
as if it was important,
as if God was fair,
as if it was really simple
if you would just be still
and bare.

TAUMARUNUI

A New Zealand Joker's Lament for his Sheila

I'm an ordinary joker getting old before my time
For my heart's in Taumarunui on the Main Trunk Line.

You can get to Taumarunui going north or going south
And you end up there at midnight and you've cinders in your mouth;

You got cinders in your whiskers and a cinder in your eye,
So you hop off at Refreshments for a cupper tea and pie
In Taumarunui, Taumarunui, Taumarunui on the Main Trunk Line.

There's a sheila in Refreshments and she's pouring cupsa tea
And my heart jumps like a rabbit when she pours a cup for me;
She's got hair a flaming yellow and a mouth a flaming red
And I'll love that flaming sheila till I'm up and gone and dead
In Taumarunui, Taumarunui, Taumarunui on the Main Trunk Line.

You can get a job in Wellington or get a job up north
But you can't in Taumarunui though you try for all you're worth;
If I want to see this sheila, then I got to take a train;
Got ten minutes for refreshments then they cart me off again
From Taumarunui, Taumarunui, Taumarunui on the Main Trunk Line.

Well, they took me on as fireman on the Limited Express,
And I thought that she'd be jake but now it's just a flaming mess;
The sheila didn't take to me; I thought she'd be a gift;

She's gone and changed her duty hours and works the daylight shift
In Taumarunui, Taumarunui, Taumarunui on the Main Trunk Line.

I'm an ordinary joker growing old before my time
For my heart's in Taumarunui on the Main Trunk Line.

BLACK BILLY TEA

Kick out your fire, boy,
Roll up your pack;
Don't forget your billy, boy,
Billy burnt and black.
Black billy tea, boy,
Black as it can be,
Black billy tea, boy,
That's the stuff for me.

Up on the snow line,
Chasing after deer,
I'd sooner have a cup o' tea
Than all your blinking beer.
Down in the coal mine,
Drivin' in a drive,
Black billy tea, boy,
Keeps a man alive.

Drink her from a tin, man,
Drink her from a cup,
Fill her up again, man,
Turn the bottoms up;
Brew it in a billy,
Brew it in a pot,
Throw in a handful,
Pour it out hot.

Mouth-organ Jack and
John the Baptist too,

The old-time swaggers
They knew how to brew.
Black billy tea, boy,
Black as Stockholm tar,
Black billy tea, boy,
Put us where we are.

Up in the bush
Getting out a log,
Upset me outfit,
In a ruddy bog.
Took out me billy,
Made a cup o' tea,
Got the outfit out again,
As easy as can be.

Used up all me ammo,
Lost me best dog,
With a Captain Cooker,
Baled up in a log.
Hauled out me billy,
Brewed her up BLACK,
Blocked up the log's end
And rolled the blighter back.

Kick out your fire, boy,
Roll up your pack;
Don't forget your billy, boy,
Billy burnt and black.
Black billy tea, boy,
Black as it can be,
Black billy tea, boy,
That's the stuff for me.

46

MONOLOGUE

I like working near a door, I like to have my work-bench
   close by, with a locker handy.

Here, the cold creeps in under the big doors, and in the
   summer hot dust swirls, clogging the nose. When the
   big doors open to admit a lorry-load of steel, conditions
   do not improve. Even so, I put up with it, and wouldn't
   care to shift to another bench, away from the big doors.

As one may imagine this is a noisy place with smoke rising,
   machines thumping and thrusting, people kneading,
   shaping, and putting things together. Because I am nearest
   to the big doors I am the farthest away
   from those who have to come down to shout
   instructions in my ear.

I am the first to greet strangers who drift in through
   the doors looking for work. I give them as much information
   as they require, direct them to the offices, and
   acknowledge the casual recognition that one worker
   signs to another.

I can always tell the look on the faces of the successful
   ones as they hurry away. The look on the faces of the
   unlucky I know also, but cannot easily forget.

I have worked here for fifteen months.
   It's too good to last.
   Orders will fall off

    and there will be a reduction in staff.
    More people than we can cope with
    will be brought in from other lands:
    people who are also looking
    for something more real, more lasting,
    more permanent maybe, than dying . . .
    I really ought to be looking for another job
    before the axe falls.

These thoughts I push away, I think that I am lucky
    to have a position by the big doors which open out
    to a short alley leading to the main street; console
    myself that if the worst happened I at least would have
    no great distance to carry my gear and tool-box
    off the premises.

I always like working near a door. I always look for a
    work-bench hard by – in case an earthquake
    occurs and fire breaks out, you know?

SECULAR LITANY

That we may never lack two Sundays in a week
One to rest and one to play
That we may worship in the liturgical drone
Of the race commentator and the radio raconteur
That we may avoid distinction and exception
Worship the mean, cultivate the mediocre
Live in a state house, raise forcibly-educated children
Receive family benefits, and standard wages and a pension
And rest in peace in a state crematorium
    Saint Allblack
    Saint Monday Raceday
    Saint Stabilisation
        Pray for us.

From all foreigners, with their unintelligible cooking
From the vicious habit of public enjoyment
From kermesse and carnival, high day and festival
From pubs, cafés, bullfights and barbecues
From Virgil and vintages, fountains and fresco-painting
From afterthought and apperception
From tragedy, from comedy
And from the arrow of God
    Saint Anniversaryday
    Saint Arborday
    Saint Labourday
        Defend us.

When the bottles are empty
And the keg runs sour
And the cinema is shut and darkened
And the radio gone up in smoke
And the sports-ground flooded
When the tote goes broke
And the favourite scratches
And the brass bands are silenced
And the car is rusted by the roadside
    Saint Fathersday
    Saint Mothersday
    Saint Happybirthday
      Have mercy on us.

And for your petitioner, poor little Jim,
    Saint Hocus
    Saint Focus
    Saint Bogus
    And Saint Billy Bungstarter
      Have mercy on him.

TELEPHONE WIRES

In the far away distance
I can hear the telephone wires
Singing in churches
Like pakehas.

THE BOMB IS MADE

The bomb is made will drop on Rangitoto.
Be kind to one another, kiss a little
And let love-making imperceptibly
Grow inwards from a kiss. I've done with soldiering,
Though every day my leave-pass may expire.

The bomb is made will drop on Rangitoto.
The cell of death is formed that multiplied
Will occupy the lung, exclude the air
Be kind to one another, kiss a little –
The first goodbye might each day last forever.

The bomb is made will drop on Rangitoto.
The hand is born that gropes to press the button.
The prodigal grey generals conspire
To dissipate the birth-right of the Asians.
Be kind to one another, kiss a little.

The bomb is made will drop on Rangitoto.
The plane that takes off persons in a hurry
Is only metaphorically leaving town,
So if we linger we will be on time.
Be kind to one another, kiss a little.

The bomb is made will drop on Rangitoto.
I do not want to see that sun-burned harbour,
Islandless as moon, red-skied again,
Its tide unblossomed, sifting wastes of ash.
Be kind to one another, kiss a little,
Our only weapon is this gentleness.

SONG IN THE HUTT VALLEY

Cirrus, stratus, cumulus,
Gentle or giant winds
Invoke the trees and cabbages;
The rising jet-trail finds
Space out of sight of valleys
Where the muddy rivers run
Past houses, groves and alleys
In the residential sun.

The placid eaves of evening
Purpled by homing sun
Pay little heed to reckoning
Broadcast by weathermen.
Houses still grow, the children
Like cabbages are seen;
Grandfather's thoughts are hidden
Upon the bowling green.

The sky's as much ambition
As anyone could eye,
Forecasts of nimbus, aeroplane
Pass over and pass by;
Tucked up at home, the passive
Who own their plot of ground
Sleep though the radio-active
Have a new formation found.

While history happens elsewhere
And few of us get hurt
Why should Grandad wish for hair
To line his sporting shirt?
His heart's at one with the children,
He can be overlooked
And left to play in the garden,
His place in heaven's booked.

The weather is established;
It will be wet – or fine –
The houses all are furnished –
In the styles of 'forty-nine.
No need to worry, hurry;
The questionmarks will keep;
The clouds and airmen marry
And the boisterous children sleep.

51

COLVILLE 1964

That sort of place where you stop
long enough to fill the tank, buy plums,
    perhaps, and an icecream thing on a stick
while somebody local comes
        in, leans on the counter, takes a good look
            but does not like what he sees of you,

intangible as menace,
a monotone with a name, as place
    it is an aspect of human spirit
(by which shaped), mean, wind-worn. Face
        outwards, over the saltings: with what merit
            the bay, wise as contrition, shallow

as their hold on small repute,
good for dragging nets which men are doing
    through channels, disproportioned in the blaze
of hot afternoon's down-going
        to a far fire-hard tide's rise
            upon the vague where time is distance?

It could be plainly simple
pleasure, but these have another tone
    or quality, something aboriginal,
reductive as soil itself — bone
        must get close here, final
            yet unrefined at all. They endure.

A school, a War Memorial
Hall, the store, neighbourhood of salt
    and hills. The road goes through to somewhere else.
Not a geologic fault
    line only scars textures of experience.
        Defined, plotted; which maps do not speak.

FOR A FIVE-YEAR-OLD

A snail is climbing up the window-sill
into your room, after a night of rain.
You call me in to see, and I explain
that it would be unkind to leave it there:
it might crawl to the floor; we must take care
that no one squashes it. You understand,
and carry it outside, with careful hand,
to eat a daffodil.

I see, then, that a kind of faith prevails:
your gentleness is moulded still by words
from me, who have trapped mice and shot wild birds,
from me, who drowned your kittens, who betrayed
your closest relatives, and who purveyed
the harshest kind of truth to many another.
But that is how things are: I am your mother,
and we are kind to snails.

DON'T KNOCK THE RAWLEIGH'S MAN

Don't knock the Rawleigh's Man
when he opens his case and offers you
mixed spices, curry powder, chilblain
ointment, Ready Relief, brilliantine,
don't say *Not now*, don't think
Piss off, but remember:
think of a hill called Tibi Dabo
behind Barcelona and the legend
that up there Satan
showed J.C. just what he was missing.
What he offered was not simply
the vulgar thing – the girls
with buttocks like mounded cream
or enough money in brewery shares
to take a Rotarian's mind off mowing lawns
for octogenarian widows,
or the sort of drink we all know
Vice-Chancellors drink when they drink
with other Vice-Chancellors –
not that but more deftly
the luciferic fingers fondled
buttons nostalgic with little anchors
as in the Mansfield story
and bits of coloured glass from old houses
and variously, these: good punctuation,
unattainable notes, throaty grunts
at bedtime, the nap of the neck

of lovely ladies caught in lamplight
like the perfect compliance of the pitch
in the last over when the last ball
takes the intransigent wicket –
yes, he did. Satan offered those things,
those were the things turned down,
that's how serious it was.
And what was round the corner as we know
was a tree already chopped
waiting to be a cross and a woman
at home rinsing a cloth white as she could
and Joseph of Arimathea still thinking the rock
he had hollowed at phenomenal expense
was going to be his, forever,
not Some Body Else's, for a spell . . .
So when the bag snaps on *your* doorstep,
flies open like leather wings
and you see instead of feathers
the tucked-in jars, the notched tubes,
the salves the spices
the lovely stuff of the flesh,
ask him in, go on, in for a moment.
There's no telling what else he might show you –
what mountain he has in mind
you may cast yourself from,
what price that your hair shimmer
like a diving hawk.

WHY DON'T YOU TALK TO ME?

Why do I post my love letters
in a hollow log?
Why put my lips to a knothole in a tree
and whisper your name?

The spiders spread their nets
and catch the sun,
and by my foot in the dry grass
ants rebuild a broken city.
Butterflies pair in the wind,
and the yellow bee,
his holsters packed with bread,
rides the blue air like a drunken cowboy.

More and more I find myself
talking to the sea.
I am alone with my footsteps.
I watch the tide recede,
and I am left with miles of shining sand.

Why don't you talk to me?

A SMALL ODE ON MIXED FLATTING

ELICITED BY THE DECISION OF THE OTAGO UNIVERSITY
AUTHORITIES TO FORBID THIS PRACTICE AMONG STUDENTS

Dunedin nights are often cold
(I notice it as I grow old);
The south wind scourging from the Pole
Drives every rat to his own hole,
Lashing the drunks who wear thin shirts
And little girls in mini-skirts.
Leander, that Greek lad, was bold
To swim the Hellespont raging cold
To visit Hero in her tower
Just for an amorous half-hour,
And lay his wet brine-tangled head
Upon her pillow – Hush! The dead
Can get good housing – Thomas Bracken,
Smellie, McLeod, McColl, McCracken,
A thousand founding fathers lie
Well roofed against the howling sky
In mixed accommodation – Hush!
It is the living make us blush
Because the young have wicked hearts
And blood to swell their private parts.
To think of corpses pleases me;
They keep such perfect chastity.
O Dr Williams, you were right
To shove the lovers out of sight;
Now they can wander half the night
Through coffee house and street and park

And fidget in the dripping dark,
While we play Mozart and applaud
The angel with the flaming sword!
King Calvin in his grave will smile
To know we know that man is vile;
But Robert Burns, that sad old rip
From whom I got my Fellowship
Will grunt upon his rain-washed stone
Above the empty Octagon,
And say – 'O that I had the strength
To slip yon lassie half a length!
Apollo! Venus! Bless my ballocks!
Where are the games, the hugs, the frolics?
Are all you bastards melancholics?
Have you forgotten that your city
Was founded well in bastardry
And half your elders (God be thankit)
Were born the wrong side of the blanket?
You scholars, throw away your books
And learn your songs from lasses' looks
As I did once –' Ah, well; it's grim;
But I will have to censor him.
He liked to call a spade a spade
And toss among the glum and staid
A poem like a hand grenade –
And I remember clearly how
(Truth is the only poet's vow)
When my spare tyre was half this size,
With drumming veins and bloodshot eyes
I blundered through the rain and sleet
To dip my wick in Castle Street,
Not on the footpath – no, in a flat,
With a sofa where I often sat,

Smoked, drank, cursed, in the company
Of a female student who unwisely
Did not mind but would pull the curtain
Over the window – And did a certain
Act occur? It did. It did.
As Byron wrote of Sennacherib –
'The Assyrian came down like a wolf on the fold
And his cohorts were gleaming in purple and gold' –
But now, at nearly forty-two,
An inmate of the social zoo,
Married, baptized, well heeled, well shod,
Almost on speaking terms with God,
I intend to save my moral bacon
By fencing the young from fornication!
Ah, Dr Williams, I agree
We need more walls at the Varsity;
The students who go double-flatting
With their she-catting and tom-catting
Won't ever get a pass in Latin;
The moral mainstay of the nation
Is careful, private masturbation;
A vaseline jar or a candle
Will drive away the stink of scandal!
The Golden Age will come again –
Those tall asthenic bird-like men
With spectacles and lecture notes,
Those girls with wool around their throats
Studying till their eyes are yellow
A new corrupt text of *Othello*,
Vaguely agnostic, rationalist,
A green banana in each fist
To signify the purity
Of educational ecstasy –

And, if they marry, they will live
By the Clinical Imperative:
A car, a fridge, a radiogram,
A clean well-fitted diaphragm,
Two-and-a-half children per
Family; to keep out thunder
Insurance policies for each;
A sad glad fortnight at the beach
Each year, when Mum and Dad will bitch
From some old half-forgotten itch –
Turn on the lights! – or else the gas!
If I kneel down like a stone at Mass
And wake my good wife with bad dreams,
And scribble verse on sordid themes,
At least I know man was not made
On the style of a slot-machine arcade –
Almost, it seems, the other day,
When Francis threw his coat away
And stood under the palace light
Naked in the Bishop's sight
To marry Lady Poverty
In folly and virginity,
The angels laughed – do they then weep
Tears of blood if two should sleep
Together and keep the cradle warm?
Each night of earth, though the wind storm,
Black land behind, white sea in front,
Leander swims the Hellespont;
To Hero's bed he enters cold;
And he will drown; and she grow old –
But what they tell each other there
You'll not find in a book anywhere.

TH BALLAD OF ROSY CROCHET

now here's a story from th timberlands I sadly have to tell
take out from it what you do think yr able
though some will say its fanciful; there's others know too well
it sure is no romance; & it aint no fable

O rosy crochet was a pretty little child
rosy crochet she knew it
rosy crochet packed a bag & ran away
she opened up th door & she went through it

her mama sd / O rosy babe / what doest thou t' me?
& she cried until th tears ran down hr shoulder
her daddy, he sd nothin: / he just let hr be
thinkin' / she'll come home before she gets much older

he ws yr average husband. O she ws yr average wife
conservative; high minded. yeah. & proper
& every thing that rosy dug throughout hr short sweet life
they put it down & they contrived t' stop her

& OFTIMES they hd MORALISED & SORELY hd predicted
that rosy wd TURN ON & so disgrace them
– dont ever smoke no GRASS they sd; – or you will get ADDICTED
(they knew th issues well; but they wd not face them)

yeah. but rosy wanted FREEDOM / she sd – I'll make it in th end!
so she split that town & got out on th HIGHWAY
& when a 22 ton timber truck came rollin' round th bend
she thumbed it / shouting / are you goin' my way?

now that truckie lost no time because there ws no time t' lose
& he LAID her with some SPEED / (also some whisky)
then she sat up front there thinkin' as she watched th world roll by
– – SHIT'S NO BIG DEAL! / it isn't even risky!

she sd – my mama's got AMPHETAMINES & daddy's got TH BOOZE
I do believe it is some kind of pity
that I cant BEND MY MIND any way I choose
– – – think I'll SCORE SOME GEAR / when I get to th city!

O she ws trying t' find some oracle that ws not ticky tacky
somethin' t' make hr cool all day; or longer
she dragged upon a KINGSIZE LOG / cd only taste tobaccy
she sd / guess I'll move along to something stronger!

so she went lookin' for a party / she went lookin' for a smoke
but th numbers on th street they did not tally
then she asked this GROOVY PUSHER in a long purple cloak
n' he sd / ah! you're stranded on ACID ALLEY

& so she rang her LOVING PARENTS. yeah. long distance telephone
she sd / 'I do not feel too well this sunday morning'
but they sd / rosy, baby, now you know YOU'RE ON YR OWN
& you're a shame unto th skin that you ws born in!

O rosy crochet; 16 saturday / 25 come monday mornin'
when that PUSHER cook'd a taste of SMACK
& brought it round hr way –
& laid it on her without any warning . . .

yeah. 'n rosy crochet; she thought she'd go away
(like many have before when all else fails)
she conned herself a ticket on th silver aeroplane
& she skipped across that ocean into N.S.W.

she got herself a habit / she got it kinda bad
she didn't have th bread t'keep it goin'
& she stood out on th street there; sold everything she had
& th cold winds from th south / they was a blowin'

& t'was there she met th JUNKIE KING straight from AFGHANISTAN
his voice ws heavy & his heart ws cold
& he stuck a dirty needle in hr alabaster arm
& he sd / 'you'd make it in AMERIKA but you're too old!'

O rosy crochet; she died yesterday
& she went out smiling like time's holy thief
& hr parents flew th body home; they knew just what t'say
though they cd SCARCE CONTAIN their PUBLIC GRIEF.

& th neighbours & relations their black suits they did hire
th undertaker's men were most decorous
& th chapel filled with singing as they roll'd her to th fire
& hr parents they sang loudest in th chorus

dont ask me if i knew her: dont ponder on hr name
dont ask me to explain; i cannot do it
i only know she groov'd in slow & gentle to hr fame
& she snatch'd a taste of FREEDOM but she blew it

& th mourners & th relatives; they all stood around
O th parson ws well fed & rolypoly
& th cemetery ws crowded when they laid hr ashes down
but th ground they laid them in; it ws not holy

& some stories are contemporary & some a long time gone
& some there are that have no end at all – –
though some say rosy stole away; some say she lingers on
when th full moon on th timberlands do fall.

REVISITING V8 NOSTALGIA

I was sitting at my writing desk
trying to work out an extra tough poem

& thinking how morbid I'd become with
words over the years, when the door

bangs open & in come two of my mates
with another guy who says (after introductions)

he's got a '54 V8 parked out front,
& would I – for old times sake – forget

the crap I'm working on & come for an
instamatic burn? . . . It's been a long time

I'm thinking as I consider the possibility
of a high speed smash with a zigzagging

pedestrian crossing . . . It's been a long time
I'm thinking as we slide into the front

seat & with a crunch roar off down
respectable montgomery avenue . . .

It's been a hell of a long time, I yell out loud
above the exhaust noise as the column

change gear-shift is banged into
second gear to take an extra fast curve . . .

& as we overtake everything in sight
down a oneway street my eyes close

as if by instinct & the car becomes a
vibrating time machine, & I see this

slick kid, D.A. hair style (not much more
than 18) behind the wheel of a

sinister-black ford '39, beerbottles rolling
in the back, fumes pouring up thru

the floorboards, tattooed arm gripping
the window ledge as if to hold the crate

together, all hell cut loose in a tightened
frightened denim jacket . . .

It's been quite a trip, I mumble — a good
8 year trip, I recall as we slide back

into respectable montgomery avenue, the
smell of fumes up my nose like 1963

perfume to a dry addict — beerbottles &
pistons rattling in my head like a bucket

of sand from a hundred resurrected
beachparties . . . For old times sake

there isn't a poem alive or dead
that's tougher than a clapped-out V8.

MAINTRUNK COUNTRY ROADSONG

Driving south and travelling
not much over fifty,
I hit a possum . . . 'Little
man,' I muttered chopping
down to second gear,
'I never meant you any harm.'

My friend with me, he himself
a man who loves such nights,
bright headlight nights, said
'Possums? just a bloody pest,
they're better dead!'
He's right of course.

So settling back, foot down hard,
Ohakune, Tangiwai —
as often blinded by
the single headlight of
a passing goods train as by
any passing car —

*Let the Midnight Special shine
its ever-loving light on me:*
they run a prison farm
somewhere round these parts;
men always on the run.
These men know such searchlight nights:

those wide shining
eyes of that young possum
full-beam back on mine,
watching me run over him . . .
'Little man,
I never meant you any harm.'

59

PATHWAY TO THE SEA

TO A.R. AMMONS

I started late summer-before-last
   digging for a
      field-tile drain
at the bottom of the garden
   where below
      topsoil that leached away
as fast as I mulched &
   fed it was
      a puggy clay

slick turning rainwater
   frost dew snow sparrow-
      piss & other seepage & drainage down
under an old shed
   in the lower adjoining
      section: here the water
bogged foundations & floorboards
   till the whole crazy
      edifice began to

settle sideways &
   slide on greased clay
      downward
taking a fouldrain with it:
   visions of 'faecal matter'
      bubbling up from clogged
overflow traps bothered
   me & some
      others too: it was time

  to act! especially since
    in addition to ordure getting
    spread around &
putting its soft mouths in
  deep cloacal
    kisses to our
livers any obvious
  breakdown in the system for
    disposal of this shit

(our shit) would
  bring the council inspectors round
    like flies
aptly, & *that* would mean
  they'd get to look at
    other aspects of how
we choose to
  live which might strike them as
    unorthodox or even

illegal: for example there's
  lots being done round here
    with demolition
timber, & that's illegal, you gotta
  use *new* timber,
    citizen, the old stuff
which was once forests of kauri &
  totara & rimu took oh
    hundreds of years to get to

    where it was when it was
        milled, the house it knit
            together stood & with-
stood 'better' than the forests
    I suppose: the timber
        served, anyway, it
did that for whoever watched
    the process through, &
        now that the houses're out

of phase much as the forests once
    were, though like the
        forests the fibre of the brittle
timber can still spring
    & ring . . . anyhow,
        now it's time
to go, it has to be stamped down, splintered
    by a dozer's tracks & what's
        left of fibre knot

& resin has a match
    put to
        it: it goes 'up
in smoke' — but round
    here we hoard the stuff &
        use it, it easily bends
nails, it splits & you
    belt your thumb often enough
        to know all about that

    but the structures
        stay put! & the inspectors
           would say 'Down
with them' — well, down with
    them! . . . I like the way you
        have to compromise with brittle
demolition timber: what gets
    built has bent the
        builder as well as his

nails & nerves: he's
    learnt something about
        service, the toughness of the
medium may have taught him
    that ease is no grateful
        index to dispensability
or availability: like
    who wants a companion for
        life or whatever span

you fancy (they're all 'for life') who can't
    put some juice
        back in your
systems? — ah how you value
    the tough lover who
        keeps you up
to the mark, whose head
    eyes language hands
        loins *en-*

gage you, give you
    elevation, a prospect, with whom you ride
        up the up &
up like birds beating on in
    the mutual updraughts of
        each other's wings – *birds*, a
subject I'll come back to later
    when I'm through with this
        drain: what needs

to be noted here, though, is that even if
    some things don't fight
        back at once or
obviously, you can still
    bet your 'sweet' (for)
        'life'
they fight back, all right & your children & children's
    children will be paying *your*
        blood-money; citizen –

well, meanwhile, we agreed, let's
    keep our shit out
        of the public eye & let's
keep our friendly sheds, our lovely slums,
    our righteous brittle screwy
        inspired constructs
up: & then
    let's add some
        flourishes, decoration in this kind

of setting doesn't coddle
   anyone, least of all the chickens
      whose coop's
included in the drainage
   problem threatening to
      overwhelm us
all: besides, we'll all
   benefit: chickens with dry
      feet lay more eggs

because they're happy: happiness
   as a concept may be
      about as brittle as
demolition timber when the latter's traced
   back to its
      forest & the former
to its causes, but it
   serves likewise, it teaches us
      'for life': if you're

for life you're for its crazy outhouses,
   the corners of happiness that don't
      square: right,
there were lots
   of reasons, the practical & the
      ideal didn't separate out,
the forests & the brittle planks
   were one, we
      were *engaged*, we wanted

to convert our drainage problem,
    transform it, *tran-*
        substantiate it, assume it into
the causes of our happiness & the
    happiness of our
        chickens whose wet feet
& poor laying rates
    rebuked us daily – we picked
        up shovels, backed off somewhat,

then we started digging fast, we went at it, we went
    down four feet & then
        two more, there was
all kinds of trash, bottles & old
    sofa springs & broken
        masonry & bricks
& unusual quantities of bones dating
    from a previous owner who'd bred
        dogs, Dobermans (-men?) 1

heard, then we began to get
    into the clay
        pug, we were out of
sight by now, the shovels hove
    into view at
        rare intervals,
shaken by
    buried handlers
        to loose the sticky glup:

    a comic & as time went by
        popular spectacle: for those
           down in the drain
the strain began to
    tell: some quit, some
        hid, some developed rheums
blisters & trenchfoot, streptococci
    swarmed upon their tonsils
        they pissed

chills straight from the kidney (it was
    now winter, autumn had
        dallied by among
the easy wreckage of an
    earlier level)
        they defected, deserted,
they offered their apologies, they
    fucked off, the practical &
    the ideal

sprang apart like
    warping unseasoned
        timber, boiiiinngg-
ggg . . . a sound, I
    thought, not
        unlike a drop
on a long rope: what
    deserters got once, & I found myself
        wishing it on them

again as I
    plied my lone shovel, bucket,
        grout, mattock, axe & spade,
baling out the boggy trench
    as the 'drainage problem' halted
        right there, hacking
through roots (that deep!) shoring
    up avalanching walls (the drain – huh! – was
        by now fifty yards

long & in some
    places twelve feet
        deep! impressive even
if left at that) & shaving
    out gummy scoops
        of clay which grunting
I then flicked heaven-
    ward into the blue
        icy sky or

alternatively into the sky
    the low colour
        of clay: clay
anyway, clay & more
    clay, the gobs landed up
        there pretty
randomly after a while, & sometimes
    they got washed
        down again by the late winter

    rain, heavy rain, which the
        roots of trees were
            sucking at, sap
    beginning to rise in them,
        refreshed by those
            surface-feeding tendrils, those deep
    tap-roots, & it's here the
        story really
            starts: not

that what's been said so far's
        irrelevant, though I apologise for its
            disorderly development &
the large number of
        seeming non-sequiturs – things
            do
follow I assure you, they
        proceed, citizen, they practically hunt
            you down, & me, who've

just been enjoying the way
        these lines unfold, much
            more easily than how the pug
& clodded
        marl left that
            drain, landing up there
out of sight & almost
        burying one
            of three baby

fruit trees (we're here) which
     therefore didn't get its tiny
          branches cut
back before the
     sap rose in them as spring came
          on gravely, gaily, with me still down
there in the trench
     still chucking the odd
          clod up & still

covering that pear tree: finally
     a retaining wall
          got built (use
was made of
     used materials) & then a truck
          came with field tiles
& another with shingle & we got
     together some
          used roofing-iron

& we had a drain! Yeah! there
     was enough fall in it to get
          'the problem' drainage
away & out of our way, the chickens
     basked & laid, the clammy surfaces
          of seeping banks
dried up, the rotting
     structures with their feet in
          clay delayed their

  inevitable demise, miasmal
    damps & soaks breathed
      out their last stinks of mould
 & fungus, artesian
    cheeps & kisses of surfacing
      wet were drowned in
birdsong, when the sun shone it
    dried & when the rain fell it ran away
      the way

we wanted: it was
    summer, the leaf
      uncrinkled from the bud
blossom fell, fruit
    spurs plumped out,
      sap circulated with its natural zest,
& one small
    pear tree, un-
      pruned, went

crazy! was a mares-nest
    of wild growth, capillary
      maze of shoots & tangled
twigs gobbling the provisions
    of root & leaf, starch
      & water, sweet open
sandwiches of rotted
    stackbottom & whatnot,
      bonbons

        & snacks broken & tasted
           by those bon-vivants the
                earthworms: the whole gusty
catering-service
      served
           that tree whose clusters
congested & grew
        together with ungainly health
           while nearby

the other two grew
        straight sturdy
           & slim, sunlight
entered their hearts,
        they reached up
           heavenwards: 'benighted' is
a word we should have
        the use of
           more often: oh pear tree! in

that condition you'd never
        score a single
           shrivelled product: well
come autumn I cut you
        back till there was almost
           nothing left: the lesson
is, effort's got to be directed . . .
        yeah, I heard
           they wanted to build an

ALUMINIUM
    SMELTER
        at
Aramoana, the sea-gate, & someone's bound to direct
    more effort that
        way soon: listen, there's
birds out there, we're
    back with those lovers, the buoyancy
        & updraught of some kind of

mutual understanding of what
    service is, of the fact that
        a thing being easy doesn't
make it available or passive:
    listen, effort's got to be right
        directed, that's
all, the catering's amazing, everything
    proceeds, citizen, sometimes
        it's hard work, but you're

engaged, you want
    to keep practical & ideal
        together, you're
for life, you know that happiness
    has to do with yes
        drains & that nature
like a pear tree
    must be served before
        it'll serve you, you

don't want your children's
   children paying
      your blood-
money, citizen, you're
   for a different sort
      of continuity, you want
to live the way
   you want
      to, you want to keep

your structures up, you
   want elevation,
      you're ready to do
your share, you'll dig your field-
   drain & you'll
      keep your shit out
of the water supply:
   you want to
      serve & to be left alone

to serve & be served,
   understanding tough
      materials, marl & old timber,
the rich claggy rind
   of the world where
      dinosaurs once
were kings: well they're gone now though
   they survived longer
      than we have

yet, but then we know, don't we,
    citizen, that there's nowhere
        to defect to, & that
living in the
    universe doesn't
        leave you
any place to chuck
    stuff off
        of.

60

WHAT NEXT?

I was kneeling in my garden, one lovely sunny morn,
I had planned a busy schedule and had commenced my task at dawn.
Bill set off with the car and trailer to take branches and hedge clippings
    to the tip
I was wishing I could have accompanied him. It is always an interesting trip.
Except for the birds chirping in the branches, the scene was peaceful and still
When all of a sudden, I had a dreadful experience, forget it I never will.
I felt a tremendous bang on my head and a sensation like a hand running
    down my back.
I thought it must be an intruder and waited in fear for another crack.
At last I mustered up courage and fearfully looked around. And to my utter
    amazement, I saw an eel lying beside me on the ground.
I thought a shag or seagull must have been flying past, with the eel held in
    its beak,
And accidentally dropped it on my head – a most extraordinary feat.
I picked it up with my spade and placed it beside me on the drive
Then I went away with my wheelbarrow, thankful to be alive.
When I returned with my load of soil the unfortunate eel was not there.
But as I was so very busy, I did not have time to care.
When Bill returned, I hurried to him, my dreadful experience to tell.
He was astonished at what I had to say, and the eel he wanted to see as well.
'Oh it's gone,' I replied, and at my words, a tender look crossed his face.
'Look here,' he said, 'You've been working too hard. Come inside and lie down
    in your favourite place.'
I was so disappointed, that he didn't believe me, but there was no proof to
    be had,
So I went back up the driveway, feeling ever so sad.
I suddenly saw a cat running quickly across the lawn next door, so I went to
    have a look and was thankful for what I saw.

There was my eel, with its head most chewed off, but enough of my evidence
    clearly in view.
So I ran down the driveway to get my husband, a most satisfactory thing to do.
My neck and shoulders were extremely sore, for days I was in pain, but I am
    quite sure that such a thing could never happen again.
Later, I was having my hair permed, and was telling my hairdresser, of my
    humorous fate,
And I said that no one would believe me, but she said that on that very date,
    she was driving to work with her husband, across the new Greenhithe
    bridge,
And watched a most interesting sight, until they passed over the ridge.
A shag was struggling in the air, with an eel held in its beak,
The eel was so huge and to handle it the shag appeared too weak.
I was so very thankful to have further evidence, that my story was true
As the shag must have given up the struggle, as over my head he flew.

ANCESTORS

Where once my ancestors grubbed for the fern's root
They build their hygienic houses now.
And where the wild pig roamed and rooted
They've measured the land into precise sections
Worth 3,000 dollars (or to sound better
For the prospective buyer, 1,500 pounds).

And here where once on an excursion up the back
Jacky pissed on a scrub
And thought no more of it
A house stands worth 10,000 (quid that is).
And where Tamati did something worse
There stands yet another house
Even more expensive than the first.

62

SHACK

I read the word shack.
I like it.
It is a good solid small word.
It would be good to live in a shack.
In inflationary times a shack
would be a good place to live.
Welcome to the shack.
It hardly exists.
You are out the exit
before you are in the entrance.
Turn it sideways —
                    it disappears.
Just a few upright bones hung with flesh.
The beating brain like a soft bunch
of kapok tossed on a derelict floor.
Love this shack, take it to your breast,
wrap your legs around it, it is the best you'll get
this year, next year, never.
Come, let us put ourselves out on the hillside,
let sunbeat drain and dry us,
windbeat drive out the loving heat,
there's more we can make
when we light up the fierce furnaces
of this rusty shack.
Let us be done with concrete and steel,
plastic and formica and all the festoonings
of luxury and comfort, all the false triptrap
gadgetry of glamour.
We can boil potatoes in the middle of the floor.

We can stoke the fire.
We can shack it.
This glorious tiny unstable living heap
which hugs the hillside.
In a week of looking for the cheapest
chintziest, ritziest, ripoff place to live in town
I got sick in the mind, sick at the heart
like Lord Randall returning to his mother
from all the agencies who own the land,
I was sick in the balls
from the way this city was dressed up,
a series of Christmas treats under the richman's
tree I wasn't allowed to unwrap.
Until I found this word shack.
I took a good bath in the word,
washed myself clean with it,
let its pure language force pour down over me
and give me back the smell
of salt and earth and iron
and the sweet wood smell burned grey by the sun.

MAKING IT OTHERWISE

I did not have a Gaelic nanny
and cannot speak the northern dialect;
no one ever said to me
that rivers were anything but water
flowing to the sea;
there was no question of tongues
licking saltern ponds like grazing beasts
or silt spread on the estuary
like a map of darkness
to be read by those
journeying towards clarity of speech.

I was raised not to know
how the spinney laid its accent on the hill
or the rain's syllables were slurred
gusting over a tin roof in the dark;
the sound of axes and children
filled every field;
trees were dropped from my curriculum;
water was water
and leaves were leaves.

Why then do I make it otherwise,
traceless in the stained tackle of the strait
saying this dried wrack
like a skeletal arm of black veins
contains everything we know?
My town has never favoured words that go
with what we see;
making them do what was not allowed
is what I take my trade to be.

64

What are known in New Zealand as grapefruit and sold to Japan as gold fruit are in fact oranges. Prior to their export to Europe and North America kiwifruit were known in New Zealand as Chinese gooseberries – and in our family as dogs' balls. In China they call them monkey peaches, except for the export trade which cans them as kiwifruit under the Greatwall and Ma Ling labels. New Zealand never did export Kiwi shoe polish, however it is manufactured there as elsewhere. As for what is sold at the Mission Safeway as New Zealand spinach I wouldn't have the foggiest. We don't grow it so far as I'm aware. There is Maori spinach, but only Maoris eat that. Like banana passionfruit, you can't buy it in the shops. You can buy tamarillos now but. We used to call them tree tomatoes.

SAD JOKE ON A MARAE

Tihei Mauriora I called
Kupe Paikea Te Kooti
Rewi and Te Rauparaha
I saw them
grim death and wooden ghosts
carved on the meeting house wall

In the only Maori I knew
I called
Tihei Mauriora
Above me the tekoteko raged
He ripped his tongue from his mouth
and threw it at my feet

Then I spoke
My name is Tu the freezing worker
Ngati D.B. is my tribe
The pub is my marae
My fist is my taiaha
Jail is my home

Tihei Mauriora I cried
They understood
the tekoteko and the ghosts
though I said nothing but
Tihei Mauriora
for that's all I knew

THE PARAKEETS AT KAREKARE

The feathers and the colours cry
on a high note which ricochets
off the monologue of the morning sun
the long winded sea, off Paratohi posturing
on a scene waiting to be painted.

Scarlet is a squawk, the green
yelps, yellow is the tightest cord
near snapping, the one high note, a sweet-sour
music not for listening. The end is
less than a step and a wink

away as the parakeet flies.
Darkness and a kind of silence under
the cliff cuts the performance,
a moment's mixture. Can scavenging
memory help itself?

What do I imagine coloured words
are for, and simple grammatical
realities like, 'I am walking to the beach'
and 'I have no idea what the sky can mean
by a twist of windy cloud'?

What's the distance between us all
as the rosella cries its tricolour
ricochet, the tacit cliff, Paratohi
Rock in bullbacked seas, my walking eye
and a twist of windy cloud?

THE NAMES

Six o'clock, the morning still and
the moon up, cool profile of the night;
time small and flat as an envelope –
see, you slip out easily: do I know you?
Your names have still their old power,
they sing softly like voices across water.

Virginia Frances Martin Rachel Stephanie
Katherine – the sounds blend and chant
in some closed chamber of the ear, poised
in the early air before echoes formed.
Suddenly a door flies open, the music
breaks into a roar, it is everywhere;

now it's laughter and screaming, the crack
of a branch in the plum tree, the gasping
and blood on the ground; it is sea-surge
and summer, 'Watch me!' sucked under
the breakers; the hum of the lupins, through
sleepy popping of pods the saying of names.

And all the time the wind that creaked in
the black macrocarpas and whined in the wires
was waiting to sweep us away; my children who
were my blood and breathing I do not know you:
we are friends, we write often, there are
occasions, news from abroad. One of you is dead.

I do not listen fearfully for you in the night,
exasperating you with my concern,
I scarcely call this old habit love –
yet you have come to me this white morning,
and remind me that to name a child is brave,
or foolhardy; even now it shakes me.

The small opaque moon, wafer of light,
grows fainter and disappears; but
the names will never leave me, I hear
them calling like boatmen far over
the harbour at first light. They will sound
in the dreams of your children's children.

WHAKATU

Eh man!
They like us on the chains
we do a good killing job
and we look so happy

    Hei tama tu tama
    tama go away

They like us in the factories
cleaning floors and shifting loads

    hei tama tu tama

they like us driving trucks and dozers
and working on the roads

    hei tama tu tama

Hey boy!
They like us in the pubs
we drink up large
and we look so happy

    Hei tama tu tama
    tama go away

E tama!
They like us
they like us
drinking & shouting & singing

when it's someone else's party
or swinging plastic pois
in a piupiu from Woolworths
and thumping hell outa an old guitar
Because we look so happy

    Hei tama tu tama
    tama go away
    Aue, tama go away.

A GAME FOR CHILDREN

Animal. Mineral. Vegetable.
The same breath sings in them all
and once the singing's over
who can distinguish the dust?

I told my sister's dog,
'Hey, dog, brush your teeth.
Wash behind your ears.
Trim your toenails.'
I warned the wedding ring,
'The game's up, you rake, you hussy!
Confess your promiscuous past.'
I stomped through Albert Park
and instructed the English trees
to pick up their messy leaves.

I threw back my shoulders.
I stood proud and erect.
I used my mussolini howl.
But all of them ignored me.
They paid no heed.
They were busy.

Animal. Mineral. Vegetable.
What does it matter?
My hair is tussock.
My bones are long stones.
I do as the dog does.

NIGHT AND NOISES

Loud nights and the creaking.
Barking voices of the dogs
   smelling around for
      fish bones.

Day comes.
The voice of a cow comes home
   for its calf.
Secretly walks through the mud
   trying to get back to its calf;
Leaning its head through
   The weta-eaten rails,
Trying to get back to its calf.

Rolling its brown glass eyes,
   Making a noise to make the
      calf answer back.

A man comes and lets the cow in
   looking in the hay pen.
The noise of the engine starts
and slowly driving the cow into the bales
To be milked and leg-roped with the rope.

Pulling the dull-coloured calf along to have a suck.

FERRET TRAP

A white hen sitting under the house
butchered, the nest cleaned out:
with a ferret about
the nights are full of noises.

They may show up in possum traps
but you're never ready, you never get
used to the noise they make when you
corner them, the smell, the coldness
of the fur to touch,
the body like a cat's surprisingly
heavy. The blood

on bait or the plate of a trap
seems darker than it ought to be,
darker than possum blood,
darker than the blood of a hen.

The dogs bark at a pair of headlights
creeping down across the black hill,
the chooks in the macrocarpa shift with unease

as you staple the trap to a wooden pile
and set it, sheep's heart jammed on a nail
for bait. You wash up, watch T.V.
and wait for the smash and the cold shrill chatter
an arm's length away from you
under the floor.

THE INVINCIBLE

From the lookout on Mt Victoria
you couldn't read their faces
but you could see how the *Invincible* dwarfed
the capital: leaning over the side
their thumbs up the same thumbs
the same bravado they took
to the Falklands.

That's the kind of image
you can put in your pocket
and take out to show people
in pubs and barber shops
I was explaining when we met
in the Pizza Express in Museum St.
We shared a Neopolitan divided
it up like the map of Africa.
I got the stereo you the bed
on through two bottles
of house wine. In between we talk art grinding
the pepper over the cheese and tomato
you say 'stuff the process I'll take
the product that's why I'm looking
forward to old age'. I think
of Gefn who Odin left because
she was too much in love
with beauty

At the next table a sailor
pushes a handle across to a woman
waiting for someone else. 'Want
a kiss or what love?' no mystery
in the invitation nothing
to make you want to look
in the mirror twice 'just sit on
my mouth love I've got a long
tongue'. He leans his arm over
her against the wall 'I'm an armourer
on liberty my hands can do amazing
things blow a hole in the bottom
of the ocean no danger pluck
a canoe out of the water
with my little finger'.

Gefn towed Zeeland into the Ocean
so she could turn the mirrors
of the world inward and Maui
who fished up these islands
was laughed to death
by a fantail.   These are the demi-
gods we understand while
No 736706 RN Armourer the *Invincible*
is stretching his hand under
the table.

THE BACK ROAD BACK

He took my baby
to a motel
in a full town
of strangers

and I stand as still
as a violet
tall in the orange hills

and the bottle is empty,
the city sparkles
like a jewel
on a scrubber's neck

It's pouring
with rain
when they board the bus
He buys
my baby
a toy
and the rain
splashes
on the window

Truck drivers
laughing past
as I come down
the back road
after my boy

It's only the
guns make
the bullets hard

I come down
the back road
Misery

It's only the
crying makes
the violets blue

and my baby's walking,
he don't look at me

a blue violet
drinking
against the orange sky

Coming down
the back road
into the land
of pain

Coming the back
road back
to hold him
again.

BLACK DRESS

I like it, second-hand, dirty and soft
I like the swing and the openings
Black dress given to me.

Who wore it? Whose waist's the same as mine?
And what say she wants it back again?

High time
she wore it.
The black's a
perfect fit.

I'd go up to anyone
dressed like this
snap my fingers and say:
Bring me sweet black tea.
I'm cold, so cold
my fingernails are blue.
Make it hot,
put rum in it
and spill it on me.

I will if you like pick up my skirts and get out
but first, speak to me. Say at least, That suits you well.
Can't you tell that I'm wearing
a material of hell.

OVER THE HARBOUR BRIDGE

Over the Harbour Bridge
On one misty morning
Went my true love Rose
To another little man.

And now I sit
And weep great tears
When I think what
I could have done
If none of it had begun.

GOING OVER THE HARBOUR BRIDGE HAPPY POEM

April is the kindest month
& I'm no fool for thinking so

look at the sea
it's just as blinding white

as summer
but there's no shrill

stink of sweat
or politicians giving you

more daylight hours
than you can comfortably handle

the banana passion fruit
are so ripe

they're walking me
homeward

& I'm sure on those white waves
there's a small boat

& on board a powerful lady
called Gertrude Stein

rowing toward Rangitoto
faster than an Evinrude —

correction: rowing toward a *painting*
hundreds of feet high

blocking off Rangitoto
just as it does in Denys Watkins' painting

& while the odd sock in my pocket
isn't taking up too much room

the trolls are dead
meaning the only thing

that stays the same
is change   and now

you can cross the harbour bridge
changeless

yet it's hard to walk right up
to the apex and leap off

whether in memory of Hart Crane
or not

but it's OK
this is a happy poem

Zac is worrying about a tuft
of hair standing up

& you are giving me
that look of love (again)

& I think it's going to be
a perfect day for banana passion fruit

Arthur the four-dogs-in-one pooch
thinks so   he's come over to say hullo

wagging the only syllable
his vocabulary allows

Arthur I'd like to tell you about the bridge
& the trolls & the odd sock in my pocket

& the tuft on Zac's head
that won't stay down

I'd like to rattle on
about the whiteness of the sea

repeating over & over
the big bright story of creation

going on right now
in April the kindest month

but you'd never believe me
– dogs have limitations

Arthur has limitations
(even though he's four dogs in one)

but this day has no boundaries
because near its beginning

I wrote
going over the harbour bridge happy poem

& from then on
it turned out pretty damn good

THELONIOUS MONK PIANO

Thelonious Monk
has just walked in the room
he's playing some sly tune
here it comes there it goes
here it comes again
you can tell it by its funny hat
Thelonious Monk plays a piano
as big as a matchbox
he's walking it & talking it
just like he always does
that's Thelonious Monk for you
shit there's more than one piano
in the room
Thelonious Monk makes music
out of aircraft carriers big floating pianos
out of refrigerators real cool pianos
out of a bus on the last trip out of town a late night piano
out of a bus on the first trip of the day a real late night piano
out of a hotel bar call it a drunk piano
out of a long distance truck call it a piano with a load
Thelonious Monk can play any kind of piano
but listening to this record you can tell
there's only one Thelonious Monk though
Thelonious Monk does the listening
his life begins to play
the memories are in his hat
the music is in his head
the ivory is in his heart
the elephant is in his fingers
walking out of Africa into the New York snow.

VIOLA

FOR GREGORY

I love the way that man
bends over his viola
drawing from it long
drapes of music –
those 'spaghetti' sounds.

Love the way he cares,
and cares! The curving
instrument submits,
taking it all on the chin.

THE DIVIDED WORLD

The world is divided between you and me, you and me babee, you and me. The world is divided between those who laugh on the inward, and those on the outward breath; between those who say at this point in time, and those who say that it does appear to be the case.

The world is divided between the superstitious, and the unimaginative; between those who love men, and those who love women; between those who have witnessed Bjorn Borg's topspin, and those who have lost the chance; between the exemplary, and the few of us who are left.

The world is divided into those who appreciate Jane Austen, and fools. The world is divided between the apathy of ignorant youth, and the despair of incorrigible old age. The world is divided between those who blame Lucifer, and those who blame a lack of dietary fibre; between mediocrity, and its own evolution; between the overworked, and the unemployed; between those who have a daughter, and those denied the greatest blessings.

The world is divided between those who say they adore the country and never go there, and those who say they hate the city and never leave it. The world is divided in the beginning, on all sides, and before God. The world is divided between those we betray, and those who betray us; between those who wake in the darkness with tears, and those too drugged to dream; between those who will not stand a dripping tap, and those who are moderate men. The world is divided amongst those who deserve it, but not often and not enough.

The world is divided between those who realize their own value, and those who think they may still amount to something; between those who prefer quiz shows, and those who still await their frontal lobotomy; between the old which has lost its edge, and the new which has not been tested; between indecision and hypocrisy, between feeble vacillation and energetic error, between cup and lip. The world is divided between those who understood the significance of Randolph Scott, and the new generation.

The world is divided between those who know nothing smoother than satin, and those who know a woman's thigh. The world is divided between the meek who will inherit the earth, and the strong who will dispossess them of it; between those who believe that they are essentially alone, and those who will be convinced with time; between Sadducees and Pharisees, Hannibal and Hasdrubal, Shaka and Dingane, Dracula and the Wolfman. The world is divided between those who make a profession of software and prosper, and those who say they recall garlands, mole-catchers and stone walls. The world is divided between silver spoons, and macrocarpa childhoods; between the appalling and the appalled; between consenting adults; between the devil, and the deep big C; between honest toiling forwards, and flashy temperamental backs; between those who help others, and those prepared to let nature take their course.

The world is divided between those who have owned a Triumph 2000, and philistines; between those who have had sex, and those prepared to give it another try; between those who remember the old school haka, and those who attend no reunions even in the mind. The world is divided between those who have a favourite corduroy coat, and those with no affection for habit. The world is divided between those who maintain the distinction between further and farther, and those who compromise with usage; between those who have attended universities, and those who have been inwardly disappointed in other ways; between animals who know only joy and pain, and we who can visualise our own deaths. The world is divided between those who can roll their tongues, and those with more archaic genes. The world is divided between those who should know better.

The world is divided between the Greeks and their gods, and the Trojans who would otherwise have won; between the Green Mountain Boys, and the Black Mountain Boys; between those who gargle in a stranger's bathroom, and those with acquired delicacy; between the undiscerning undistinguished undeserving mass, and us. The world is divided into the states of Jeopardy and Paranoia, Halidom and Dugong, Condominium and the Tribal Lands, all of these, none of these. The world is divided between those who try themselves, and those who seek a less corrupt judge.

The world is divided between those who are tolerant and wise, and their husbands. The world is divided between those in authority, and those resentful of it; between those who are white, and those whose virtues are not so immediately apparent; between those who face the world with a religion, and those who wish to but have only irony in its place. The world is divided between those who have shifted to the North Island, and those passed over for promotion; between one thing and another if distinctions should be made; between tolerant contempt of the artist, and awe of the Cactus and Succulent Society's President. The world is divided between a lawyer and his client, but not equally or *per se*.

The world is divided between those people whose character is known, and those from whom something may still be expected. The world is divided between rancour and disgust, idolatry and idiocy, ballet and bidet, Sordello and Bordello, Bishop Blougram's and Prufrock's apologies. The world is divided between the first and the last; between a man and a woman; between the sun and moon; stoics and epicureans; scholars and dullards; the fragrance of mint in the riverbeds and desolate clay. The world is divided between Lucky Jims, and those who see no humour in it; between professed intentions, and the things we would wish undone; between nostalgic falsehood, and anticipatory regret; between dreams of avarice, and visions of self-esteem.

The world is divided between the vices of free will, and the virtues of necessity; between those who know where be Wold Jar the tinker, and those cast into darkness; between those who delight in games, and those who lack even that saving grace; between Tyrannosaurus Rex, and civilized marriages; between New Zealanders, and those people with a culture; between our adult selves, and the blue remembered hills.

The world is divided between those who boast of their climate, and those who rejoice in secret that a cold wind isolates a landscape. The world is divided between those who accept the division, and those who instigated it; between books on the Royal Family or gardens and the remaining ten percent of publishers' products; between those who are proud, and those who have lost their self-respect and so become the most dangerous of men. The world is divided on the merits of everything; on all questions raised (at this point in time). The world is divided between optimism, and Mr Weston's good wine; between those who see, and those who understand; between confiding voluble people, and those we wish to know; between those on the inside looking out, and those on the outside looking in.

The world is divided between men who despise others for being what they are, and women who despise them for what they are not. The world is divided between those anxious concerning the physical and those in terror of the mind; between those who love sausages and onions, and those who are effete; between the people we always suspected, and the butlers who did it; between idlers, and those who work hard all their lives to be able to do nothing when they die.

The world is divided between the few now, and the great majority on the other side. The world is divided above all, while we sleep, beneath our noses, and before we notice. The world is divided as we are all divided. The world is divided between you and me, you and me for a time, you and me.

COMPULSORY CLASS VISITS

they come in classes now
many pakeha ones too
and even the maori start to call themselves
new zealanders.
and even the maori stand on the marae saying 'this is the only place
you can be maori on.'
it is not enough for me.
the young are in constant challenge with the middle-aged,
the men who take their teeth out.

at the powhiri they are directed to sing
there is no kaea there is no ihi.
holding their papers, they look at the words –
Ao – te – a – roa.

81

POSTCARD

Opening a refrigerator,
you find Port Chalmers.
Now and then a little light comes on.
Two bottles of milk are white breasts
in the fists of a milkman.
In the dairy
a member of the counter culture grinds the Turkish blend.
A fly reads the fine print on a fishtail.
Rain is a sad lover,
chucking cheap beads onto the cemetery grass.
Sparrows disco dance in the trees above.
The wind vacuums the flash Wool Board carpet
of the sea.
Later, the sunlight tenderly bandages a wounded look.

VANILLA RIM

white sky
vanilla rim
mountains

rake ginger
trash under
trees avenues

tastes sweet
difficult
on the tongue

see though
gone thinning
air 'bouton

boutonnière:
everything
flowers' that

old was sung
walks hard
around it

CHEVY

Just what you've come to expect
of civilisation, beside
the road, down a bank,
veined with vines

and a net of old man's beard,
a rusting wreck, a
Chevy of the kind
we used to ride in

over 30 years ago – Mum,
Dad, me, and my younger
brother. We felt we'd
arrived; it gave us

the novelty of status,
America's showy opulence
revealing itself to us,
slow starters, hicks

way down in the remotest
reaches of the South Pacific.
It was a key, a chariot
of the real world.

So there was a great old
Chevy, two doors
missing, windscreen gone
leaving one wiper blade

like a feeler
waving. Only one rear wheel
remained and the upholstery
gaped at us.

On the back seat
my son found
a yellowy paperback Western
about Zane Croker

and a whole heap of trouble
at the B-Bar-B; and also
a condom that had seen
better days. He smiled,

picked it up, and
asked me what it was.
He looked me straight in the eye
while I told him.

84

FOR BOB ORR, AGAIN

A week's absence – you'll choke;
I return to my room this morning
to find the only thing left
an immovable Underwood 'writer

I'd defy you to want to pinch.
They tell me I laugh in my sleep.
Well, I have a brother of whom I'm fond.
I dreamed him dead the other night,

As firm in death as apples.
Youth, beauty, Easter fucking Island;
That's the quality of dream you get nowadays,
laughter or not.

Construct instead a pyramid of strings,
an airy cage of lines, as merely lines
as maps or atlases, to sharpen razors in.
And live in it I reckon, Bob.

A CORTÈGE OF DAUGHTERS

A quite ordinary funeral: the corpse
unknown to the priest. The twenty-third psalm.
The readings by serious businessmen
one who nearly tripped on the unaccustomed pew.
The kneelers and the sitters like sheep and goats.

But by some prior determination a row
of daughters and daughters-in-law rose
to act as pallbearers instead of men
all of even height and beautiful.
One wore in her hair a black and white striped bow.

And in the midst of their queenliness
one in dark flowered silk, the corpse
had become a man before they reached the porch
so loved he had his own dark barge
which their slow moving steps rowed
as a dark lake is sometimes surrounded by irises.

NORTHERN OAKS

Dry leaves crush
underfoot in lush

grass smooth
pinnacles nest against
a grey

spire

the trunks seem to leap
from earth like whales

o

Low broken cloud maps
astonishment. Cattletrucks roar

along the outfield, seagulls
romp down the sky
adjusting their feet
like cats in mid-air

o

Freshly conditioned toetoe
a faded advertisement for NewJoy

icecream. Young women enter
the summer evening wearing
racquets on their shoulders

WE LISTEN FOR YOU ON THE RADIO

We know that there is
a yacht out there
struck into our map,
a star disabled north of Cape Reinga.
The cyclone blows it backwards
so that the land is
two hundred miles away; more than that.

You are out there
and the sea
will find its way into your ears
and mouth, it
fills your eyes with salt.
And *land* is somewhere.
You hold it in front of your eyes

in the small place that is safety
and walking down the street,
slow walking soft *light*,
your lover curled into the
small of your back,
a child clinging to the tips
of your fingers,

and the apples falling from the tree,
rotting in the yellow grass.
You can't see the horizon and
your life passes in the
time it takes to fall from
the top of a wave
and rise to the next,

and you fall fall fall
an eternity of apples
falling,
and the breaking of
branches.
The face of the next wave
is the face of your lover.

You have never seen
anything like it (these waves).
The sea will swallow you
if you don't get it right,
straight up the face, tremble
on the eyelash of the wave –
down the nose and into the hungry

mouth where it is hollowed,
still.
(Your child)
The branch snapped
and she fell
cried and you were there
with comfort and you

bound and soothed, held her
in your arms.
(The ribs are sprung,
the water finds its way in)
and we hear your voice crackle
out of phase down the radio,
the child and I.

(If you had two arms you would
hold us both.)
We cling to each other
even as you cling to the back
of your life,
cling to the few words that tell us
you are somewhere out there alive,

with three broken ribs,
running hills and valleys
our photograph safe inside your oilskin.
That you are alive,
eking out a can of spaghetti
some biscuits,
plumbing the wet chart

the face of land, the face
of each new wave mountain.
Time stops, three more days
of gale force winds
crawl on their bellies towards
you.
We don't know if you can

hear us, we can hear you.
We watch the tiny star which gives
your position make its way
down the TV screen on the
six o'clock news.
Your face is a little square
on the front page of The Sun.

The ends of bone crunch each other.
The radio threads you in
to us, then there is silence.
We would have the land moved
for you,
peeling back contours, licking
them and sticking an entire island

down,
its outline for you to step off
onto *land*.

88

MAKE SURE

Make sure you fall in love with a man who you know will survive in the bush. This way, when he is three nights overdue from his trip and the search and rescue team is out looking for him and the helicopter has been called back because the weather is closing in and they're interviewing you on television in a close-up camera shot, asking you what you think his chances are – hoping you will cry and your lip will tremble – you can look them straight in the eye and say you *know* he will be all right, he has had plenty of experience and he knows what to do, he was carrying plenty of food and warm clothing and he is strong.
Even if he is hurt, you know he will be all right.
He's a fighter, you'll say. He won't give in.
But the weather is closing in, you must be worried, they'll ask.
You keep your resolve. He will be all right, you say.
I know he will.

THE BLUES

The lights are on all over Hamilton.
The sky is dark, blue
as a stained glass window in an unfrequented church
say, by Chagall, with grand and glorious chinks
of pinks and purples,
glittering jewels on those glass fronted buildings
where the lifts are all descending
and the doors are
being closed.
                You're out there somewhere,
going to a concert in wide company or maybe
sitting somewhere weaving a carpet
like a giant tapestry, coloured grey,
pale brown, weaving the wool
back in at the edges of the frame, your
fingers deft as they turn the wool in tight and
gentle curves.
              Or somewhere else.
What do I do
except imagine you?
The river I keep crossing
keeps going north. The trains
in the night cross it too.
Their silver carriages are blue.

CABIN FEVER

Three weeks of cyclone weather, and we're all starting
to get a bit scratchy. From Vancouver my brother writes
that he's practising for global warming. Rain every day for
weeks. On CBC Stereo they're predicting a green Christmas;
further east the live Xmas tree companies will be going belly

up. Can you blame them? Here at least I can still get out
and run, even in rain, I tell myself, even in a thirty knot
easterly. Have you noticed the sound of rain on a Moreton
Bay fig, for instance, Captain Fyans? Dry and pellety. Or
the way the black ones grunt and snort as the wind lashes

them, as though they're alive? See, now that we're out here,
how it is the tracks in the park fill up first with water,
down there on the edge of the paddock, or up here, on the lawns.
Not that I run this way much, not since the car backed up, and I
took off in the dusk like a rabbit, running towards the light.

Six of them. I'd have had no show. Today I stay clear of the road,
take a note of parked cars and moving ones, and plan my route
towards the houses in case of trouble. From a distance the mutter
of the city rises towards me. *Times were simpler, once; given
a length of four by two and some fencing wire a bloke could invent*

*anything really, art unions, smoko, ladies a plate, all your major
social institutions, race relations included.* Sheilas didn't run,
either – away or for any other reason. So you could say they,
i.e. the jokers in the car, were only trying to reclaim
the recent past using what was near, and served. It all depends

on where you're looking from. The country viewed from an Air New Zealand F27 on a misty winter morning, might just resemble a J boat, very broad in the beam, sailing bravely south away from Europe and towards the ice, or a waka, small as a room, unstable in a big swell, blown off course and heading nowhere in particular.

PROPOSAL AT ALLANS BEACH

Basalt capes
thrust into the sea, the sea
curls back intimately
into the land, celebrating
a moody marriage. The wind here
saws into flesh like cord
but just around the sandhills
a small inland sea
dotted with maimais calmly sends
the sun back to heaven.
Even in winter you can lie
on its hard white beach
naked as if you'd just crawled
up from the sea like a fish with legs
and were looking around for a mate.
But up there above the ridges
it's always going on: the air
dividing, and pouring mist
down ngaio gullies, making sheep
get up and move, unveiling contours
taking them away again.
The whole place is a test site.
I've been bringing
people here for 20 years –
sometimes with a hard question
mostly to see how we match up
to its absolute background.
It never fails. Walk with someone
from the flax-hung cliff at one end

to the tidal creek at the other
and you'll know for sure
what's biting both of you
whether you could be friends for life
and lesser domestic truths. Of course
I had to be brought here once myself
on a particularly uninviting day.
Squinting up the dark green slopes
I knew I'd come home. Later
I sat by the lagoon a whole
sunfilled September day and planned
the work of a decade. And once
I came here with a friend and the rain
blew back into our faces and told us
we could never be the lovers
we thought we wanted to be.
I'm never alone here –
the place is full of ghosts.
With luck, you might see one
swimming naked in a rock pool
on the greyest day of the year.
It is a place for strong attachments:
friends, lovers, children.
I can't promise much
but you won't forget having been here
nor who you came with, and all
that followed, if it followed.

BOWL

FOR VIV

I
You carry the bowl around
in your head till one day
the block jolts.
     You press
the grain against the lathe,
fiercely, gently. The bowl
is well aware of its own
shape,
   a hemisphere of honey
light, flawed to perfection.
You go back & back to the same
leaping off place.

II
      Falling in love
is a 'genetically instinctual
component of mating behaviour.'
Falling in love is shapelessness,
a collapse of boundaries.
      The bowl
takes a bite out of the white
window frame.
     It has shed the grand
& shaggy gestures of a tree. Compact
now, it pulls itself together,
alert, passionate, reticent.

III
           Miracles are a matter
of timing, grace is routine.
Run your fingers on the lip
of the bowl round & round
without end.
           Gradually
you will come to the place
where you know what you are doing.

NO PROBLEM, BUT NOT EASY

This is the Green Man
He lives at the corner of Hello Street and Goodbye.
He lives in a house, Alchemy House.

When you stand close to him
He is surely a man, you can see that
Sometimes, even, he has a beard.

And there are times when you see him
From afar, say, from across the room
He is also a woman.

Now, she is the Green Woman.
This is the way it is.

Sometimes he is friendly
Always in a hurry to be singing.
Sometimes she is not unfriendly
She is full of lightness, and music.

And there are times when he is quite terrible
Full of fire, you had better watch out.
And sometimes she is quite bossy
Even wicked, be careful.

Which is the way it is.

And you know, sometimes even they go to war.
There is destruction all over the place.

And of course there are times
When they lie down in each other's arms
And they touch each other again and again.

And this is the way it is:
No problem, but not easy.

I WAS A FEMINIST IN THE EIGHTIES

To be a feminist you need to have
a good night's sleep.

To be a feminist you need to
have your consciousness raised
and have a good night's sleep.

To be a feminist you need to
have regard for your personal well-being
have your consciousness raised
and have a good night's sleep.

To be a feminist you need to
have a crack at financial independence
have regard for your personal well-being
have your consciousness raised
and have a good night's sleep.

To be a feminist you need to
champion women, have a crack at
financial independence, have regard
for your personal well-being
have your consciousness raised and
have a good night's sleep.

To be a feminist you need to do the
childminding, washing, shopping, cooking and cleaning
while your mind is on higher matters
and champion women, have a crack

at financial independence, have regard
for your personal well-being
have your consciousness raised
and have a good
night's sleep.

To be a feminist you need to button
your coat thoughtfully, do the childminding
washing, shopping, cooking and cleaning
while your mind is on higher matters
and champion women, have a crack at
financial independence, have regard for
your personal well-being, have your
consciousness raised and have
a good night's
sleep.

To be a feminist you need to
engage in mature dialogue with
your spouse on matters of domestic
equality, button your coat thoughtfully
do the childminding, washing, shopping, cooking and cleaning
while your mind is on higher matters
and champion women, have a crack at
financial independence, have regard
for your personal well-being, have
your consciousness raised and
have a good
night's
sleep.

Then a lion came prowling out of the jungle
and ate the feminist all up.

THE SMELL OF HER HAIR

i thought it an elusive citrus
but he said
'that's the scent from the yellow knob
on a wild duck's bum'

wild duck
and picked her up
'why aren't you a boy?' he said
and breathed her hair

BUBBLE TROUBLE

Little Mabel blew a bubble and it caused a lot of trouble . . .
Such a lot of bubble trouble in a bibble-bobble way.
For it broke away from Mabel as it bobbed across the table,
Where it bobbled over Baby, and it wafted him away.

The baby didn't quibble. He began to smile and dribble,
For he liked the wibble-wobble of the bubble in the air.
But Mabel ran for cover as the bubble bobbed above her,
And she shouted out for Mother who was putting up her hair.

At the sudden cry of trouble, Mother took off at the double,
For the squealing left her reeling . . . made her terrified and tense,
Saw the bubble for a minute, with the baby bobbing in it,
As it bibbled by the letter-box and bobbed across the fence.

In her garden, Chrysta Gribble had begun to cry and cavil
At her lazy brother, Greville, reading novels in his bed.
But she bellowed, 'Gracious, Greville!' and she grovelled on the gravel,
When the baby in the bubble bibble-bobbled overhead.

In a garden folly, Tybal, and his jolly mother, Sybil,
Sat and played a game of Scrabble, shouting shrilly as they scored.
But they both began to babble and to scrobble with the Scrabble
As the baby in the bubble bibble-bobbled by the board.

Then crippled Mr Copple and his wife (a crabby couple),
Set out arm in arm to hobble and to squabble down the lane.
But the baby in the bubble turned their hobble to a joggle
As they raced away like rockets . . . and they've never limped again.

Even feeble Mrs Threeble in a muddle with her needle
(Matching pink and purple patches for a pretty patchwork quilt),
When her older sister told her, tossed the quilt across her shoulder,
As she set off at a totter in her tattered tartan kilt.

At the shops a busy rabble met to gossip and to gabble,
Started gibbering and goggling as the bubble bobbled by.
Mother, hand in hand with Mabel, flew as fast as she was able,
Full of trouble lest the bubble burst or vanish in the sky.

After them came Greville Gribble in his nightshirt, with his novel
(All about a haunted hovel) held on high above his head,
Followed by his sister, Chrysta (though her boots had made a blister),
Then came Tybal, pulling Sybil, with the Scrabble for a sled.

After them the Copple couple came cavorting at the double,
Then a jogger (quite a slogger) joined the crowd who called and coughed.
Up above the puzzled people – up above the chapel steeple –
Rose the bubble (with the baby) slowly lifting up aloft.

There was such a flum-a-diddle (Mabel huddled in the middle),
Canon Dapple left the chapel, followed by the chapel choir.
And the treble singer, Abel, threw an apple core at Mabel,
As the baby in the bubble bobbled up a little higher.

Oh, they giggled and they goggled until all their brains were boggled,
As the baby in the bubble rose above the little town.
'With the problem let us grapple,' murmured kindly Canon Dapple,
'And the problem we must grapple with is bringing baby down.'

'Now, let Mabel stand on Abel, who could stand in turn on Tybal,
Who could stand on Greville Gribble, who could stand upon the wall,
While the people from the shop'll stand to catch them if they topple,
Then perhaps they'll reach the bubble, saving baby from a fall.'

But Abel, though a treble, was a rascal and a rebel,
Fond of getting into trouble when he didn't have to sing.
Pushing quickly through the people, Abel clambered up the steeple
With nefarious intentions and a pebble in his sling!

Abel quietly aimed the pebble past the steeple of the chapel,
At the baby in the bubble wibble-wobbling way up there.
And the pebble *burst* the bubble! So the future seemed to fizzle
For the baby boy who grizzled as he tumbled through the air.

What a moment for a mother as her infant plunged above her!
There were groans and gasps and gargles from the horror-stricken crowd.
Sibyl said, 'Upon my honour, *there's* a baby who's a goner!'
And Chrysta hissed with emphasis, 'It shouldn't be allowed!'

But Mabel, Tybal, Greville, and the jogger (christened Neville)
Didn't quiver, didn't quaver, didn't drivel, shrivel, wilt.
But as one they made a swivel, and with action (firm but civil),
They divested Mrs Threeble of her pretty patchwork quilt.

Oh, what calculated catchwork! Baby bounced into the patchwork,
Where his grizzles turned to giggles and to wriggles of delight!
And the people stared dumbfounded, as he bobbled and rebounded,
Till the baby boy was grounded and his mother held him tight.

And the people there still prattle – there is lots of tittle-tattle –
For they glory in the story, young and old folk, gold and grey,
Of how wicked treble Abel tripled trouble with his pebble,
But how Mabel (and some others) saved her brother and the day.

FAST COLD

There's a damp facecloth in the front of our skulls that sits between two sprung clamps. Unhappiness releases the springs so the clamps push together, forcing water out of the cloth. The only way out for this water is through the eyes, and it runs down our faces, washing them.

Teenage boys are made to practise holding their eyes tightly closed at such times so the water is forced back into the skull. Only some of this water can be reabsorbed by the facecloth. The rest sloshes about in the hollow beneath, slowly rusting the mechanism, until it ends up not working at all.

HOW TO TALK

It was on the ferris wheel
I was introduced to

the art of conversation.
She was thirteen,

I was fourteen;
many times we passed the point where we'd climbed on.

How high it is, up here, she said
when we were near the top.

I could see my name
on the tip of her tongue.

MY FATHER'S STUTTER

Struck at certain times as when his mother
interrupted him or at the quick demands
his older brothers made. We kids, too, knew
how to force it, though that was a terror
of its own as if someone had him by his great
singer's throat. Otherwise he lectured quite
happily, growing lucid the further into molecular
structure he got.

There was also his part-time opera
career and the endless afternoons of
rehearsals we were taken to. His big smooth
chorus bass shaking our best seats in
the house. The same Italian phrases
sounding over and over on
over our heads.

And now just recently I have noticed odd
impediments in my own words. Nothing
to snap my head back but false starts, beginnings
of wild alliteration. Not so smart. A programming
thing though I tell myself I am growing into it, slowly
and from dislike, as I work at his music;
the crowd scene – his favourite – in La Bohème when all the
bohemians, I guess they are, rush about, sing
at once and from the talky noise emerges – there!
Tune.

AT THE GRAVE OF GOVERNOR HOBSON

You started it all. Here for you it ended.
Here it goes on. A bridge over Grafton Gully
casts morning shadow. A motorway shaves the graveyard
and crops it back. Through oaks and undergrowth
the interrupted light on broken gravestones
writes and erases itself. Further down
was once a stream. Sometimes a former someone,
drunk, derelict, or dead by misadventure,
was found there. It was our forest in the city
with paths and dangers – most of it now cut down.

Immemorial aunts, great uncles, cousins
I'm told are here. A still decipherable headstone
remembers my forebear who walked behind your coffin
and five years later joined you under the oaks.
Your children went back to England. We remained
to inherit your city, and that distrusted Treaty
you made as instructed by those who would later call it
'little more than a legal fiction'. Your dearest Liz
took home her title to two hundred Auckland acres,
prospered, a widow in Plymouth, and didn't remarry.

Shadow pickets fall on the raised white slab
that marks your grave. A Caribbean pirate
once put a noose to your neck, then changed his mind
and set you adrift without sail. You lived to die
at a desk in a dream of Auckland, clouded by

headaches that came from the south. A riderless horse
was led behind the coffin eight sailors carried.
All day the tribes lamented. 'Send us no boy,'
a Chief wrote to the Queen, 'nor one puffed up,
but a man good as this Governor who has died.'

'Remote,' they called it; 'lacking natural advantage.'
That you chose the Waitemata, that your choice attracted
artisans from the south, that from this site
you asserted your right to govern – these were facts
the Wakefields wouldn't forgive. 'It is not my purpose,'
you wrote, 'that I should disparage Port Nicholson,
but only, against deceptions, to say that I find
here a more genial climate, more fertile soil.'
No people chooses its history. Doubting our own,
we can say at least in this we know you were right.

Our chopper-cops go over, eyeing Auckland.
From a car radio a voice I'm sure belongs
to Kiri Te Kanawa skies itself through branches
with 'Let the Bright Seraphim'. Under the bridge
Maori street-kids have tuned their ghetto-blaster
to Bobby Brown. A boy sniffs glue from a bag
beneath his jacket. Messages on the arch
in well-schooled spray-can read 'King Cobras Rule'
and 'The Treaty is a Fraud'. Governor, all about you
for better and worse, your memorial goes on growing.

Last night, yellow as butter, an outsize moon
sailed over the ridge of Parnell. In Emily Place
it picked the obelisk out that marks the place
where you laid the first stone for the first St Paul's;
it gilded the six-lane highway, once a track,

where you used to lead your Lila and her schoolfriend
Harriet Preece, and lift them over the ditch;
it laid a lily of light on 'this beautiful plot
on the slope of a wooded valley looking to the sea',
once yours and, given to the city, yours again.

Let today be all the days we've lived in New Zealand:
stench of whale-meat, a rat cooked on a spit,
morning boots frozen hard, the southern Maori
ravaged by measles, rum, Te Rauparaha;
wars in the north, gumfields, forests falling
to ruminant grassland, cities climbing like trees;
and everywhere this language both subtle and strong.
You didn't start it, Governor. As we do, you fashioned
what time, and the times that live in us, required.
It doesn't finish. These verses have no end.

THE HISTORIAN

They watch from the shadows of the bank
crouched over cold embers
they suck the fat from the sand
staring through the mangled roots of pohutukawa
they are the Maori dead
their mouths are filled with sand.

In the tremulous light of the driftwood fire
he casts his nets, drawing the women to him
he speaks on matters of consequence; he speaks
of contexts and correlatives; expels from his nose
a last wisp of cigar smoke
with a decisive snort.

As we walk up the sand path
he cleaves the night with an anecdotal arm.

Entering the bach we are rinsed
in fluorescent light, the darkness washed from us
the women are cooking the catch of the day
plates of piper and paua and scallops
lift his voice, unsteady his hand, bring the glass to his lips
his cheeks glow brighter as his eyes lose light.

Down on the beach the Maori dead
are talking among themselves
their faces are streaked with fat and charcoal
on their tongues loll translucent pupae
they speak of travel, they speak
of fishing grounds in the north, of Moehau, of Hahei.

He steps back into the night, admitting
a sudden gasp of surf.

On the beach the Maori dead
loll in the tide, faces slurred limbs dissolving
into black water
their shoulders are draped with bull kelp, lice
skim through the holes of their eyes
they dive for paua to fill their porous bellies.

A door closes. I hear the creak of floorboards.
Hushed voices. Creak of a camp bed.

CONCRETE

In the weeks before he laid the path
to the front door
and put in steps
from the side entrance to the basement

he went to the library and borrowed a manual
sat weekends at a website
and talked at length in his lunch hour
with others
who had made the journey before him.

'Concrete's a male thing,' he said
'we appreciate the details of durable materials
the comparative benefits of embedded metals

and the step-by-step techniques
by which reinforced steel
in the form of rods, bars, or wires
can be stretched and retracted
to predetermined limits

better than you do

blokes can relate to it
we have a sense of it

there's a lot more to concrete
than the bonding
of sand and water
with stone and cement

there's a history of structural form to consider
think of the lighthouse
after oil lamps, torches, and antiquity

I'm talking about isolated rocks
exposure to the sea
strength without mass

a slender tower
a spiral base
and a design which allows a cylinder
to be set in the sea

think of the way it sets
around the tautly drawn wire
in the curves
and reinforced spans
of the world's major bridges

think of the classical example
of the Colosseum
iron clamps in its joints
enclosed on all sides

and the small volume of poems
around 80 AD
which celebrated its construction.
There are correlations,' he murmured

'between concrete
cubism
and the visual construction of verse

you can make a poem
out of concrete items
like iron
or eggshells

in the case of rain
you can let the letters fall in long slanting lines

consider e.e. cummings
famous for his typographical eccentricities

or the visually innovative man
in his workshop

making goddesses for the garden
and gnomes
with knives in their backs
he is doing a similarly tangible thing
I'm told that his aliens
Mexicans
and tyre-marked opossums
are popular

that people have been known
to write the names of their pets
on the necks of the replicas
he makes for them

but perhaps I'm straying nearer to philosophy here –
concrete as distinct from abstract
it's an interesting area –

concrete as real life
concrete as a bird
balanced with precision
on the uppermost branch of a tree

as a boy riding a skateboard

as existential experience

as concrete as rigid paving

this could mean we are talking
vegetation clearing
earthmoving
graders and bulldozers

the size and weight of traffic using the highway

the possibility
of underground streams

a system by which we can carry rainwater
to shallow gutters
at the edge of the shoulder

and the likelihood of erosion
if the steps are cut
into the wrong sort of hillside

in which case
we'll need a building code
for the slope

and a plan of action
should ground water drain
down the back of the section

and the earth start to slip
in the absence
of a retaining wall.

Look at this diagram —
sub-base
compaction
and a layer of concrete —

it raises questions of
shrinkage
temperature control

and warping of the slab
due to moisture variations
between top and bottom

and means that
on a summer's day

hosing of the garden
or lawn
on either side of the pathway

or more particularly
the steps

could lead to
cracking
crumbling

and the undignified sight
of concrete
losing its grip on the hillside.'

*

His path to the front door
was an unqualified success.

Later, he built the steps
to the basement

and every one of them
was unique.

WE DON'T KNOW HOW LUCKY WE ARE

At the dawn of the day in the great southern ocean
When the world's greatest fish was being landed
And the boat they were pulling it into was sinking
And the sea was quite lumpy and the weather was foul
And the bloke with the map was as pissed as an owl
And the boys called out 'Maui you clown, let it go',
In the noise he reached down for his grandmother's jawbone
And winked at his mates and said 'Boys . . .

    We don't know how lucky we are
    I've a feeling I have stumbled on something substantial'
    We don't know how lucky we are
    We don't know how lucky we are

I was speaking to a mate of mine
Just the other day
A guy called Bruce Bayliss actually
Who ah, lives up our way
He's been away on a 'round the world Eighth Army do'
For a year, more or less
I said 'describe the global position Bruce?'
He says 'Fred it's a mess

    We don't know how lucky we are in this country
    We don't know how lucky we are'
    We don't know how lucky we are
    We don't know how lucky we are

There's a guy I know, who lives in town
I see him about once a year I s'pose
He's had a coronary since Easter
He's got a haemorrhage in his ear
He went bankrupt a couple of weeks back
And now his wife's left him too
I said 'You're looking odd mate, you're looking queer
What are you going to do?'

    He says 'We don't know how lucky we are, to live in this joint,
    We don't know how lucky we are' he repeated
    We don't know how lucky we are
    We don't know how lucky we are

So when things are looking really bad
And you're thinking of giving it away
Remember New Zealand's a cracker
And I reckon come what may
If things get appallingly bad
And we're all under constant attack
Remember we want to see good clean ball
And for God's sake feed your backs

    We don't know how fortunate we are to have that place
    We don't know how propitious are the circumstances, Frederick
    We don't know how lucky we are
    We don't know how lucky we are
    We don't know how lucky we are
    We just don't realise how fortunate we are
    We've no idea of the luck we possess, collectively
    We just don't know how lucky we all are

WAKA 99

If waka could be resurrected
they wouldn't just come out
from museum doors smashing
glass cases revolving and sliding
doors on their exit

they wouldn't just come out
of mountains as if liquidified
from a frozen state
the resurrection wouldn't just
come about this way

the South Island turned to wood
waiting for the giant crew
of Maui and his brothers
bailers and anchors turned back
to what they were when they were strewn

about the country by Kupe
and his relations
the resurrection would happen
in the blood of the men and women
the boys and girls

who are blood relations
of the crews whose veins
touch the veins who touched the veins
of those who touched the veins
who touched the veins

who touched the veins
of the men and women from the time
of Kupe and before.
The resurrection will come
out of their blood.

MARTON

We're at the Golf Club discussing satanic cults.
They had a special day for the young people
who committed suicide under the Marton bridge.
As if we haven't got enough tragedies in cars.
We had bodgies and widgies, but they were harmless.
The line dancers were upset
because the stage was uneven.
It was just plain dangerous.
The man in the ice-cream van thought the line dancing
music was the best he had heard all day.
All of these young people are growing up without melody.
They just like improvising noise. And when they sing
you can't make out the words.
Anyone would think they were in pain.
Did you go? God, no!
They've got four televisions in the TAB
and I could still hear it.
The Karate Club put on a display. But they'd forgotten to organise
something to kick.
There's been four youth groups set up since the war.
They've all started with a hiss and a roar.
One boy was eating his girlfriend.
There were little kids there.
The Mayor made a plea to the young folk of the Rangitikei:
'Please stop dying.'
I sit on the verandah and watch them walk home from school,
smoking and swearing. I wouldn't cross the road
to kick them up the arse.
I blame the parents.

I'm glad someone said that.
The TV came and talked to Gypsy
only because he had tattoos on his face
and some other guy, no one knew,
who was totally out of it,
lying in the grass in his leathers.
There were ordinary people there too.
It's supposed to become an annual thing.

WHY OUR WASHING MACHINE BROKE

On the first day of school I missed my mother. I had home-made beef-roast sandwiches but I missed her. There she was at home-time and it was all okay, all of it.

On the second day of school, I missed my mother. I had home-made beef-roast sandwiches but I still missed her. At home-time she was five minutes late but it was all still okay, it was all pretty much okay.

On the third day of school it was making me cry. There was no beef-roast today and the school lunches tasted yucky. My mother came at home-time but the luncheon taste was in my mouth, pinky smelly luncheon and it tasted yuck.

On the fourth day of school they gave me poison. I am sure of it. I was sick all day and sick when I got home. My teacher said it was nothing. My mother said it would pass. The poison said, eat me, eat me all up.

The next day of school I got very confused. When I tried to draw a seagull it just looked like a straight line and I didn't understand how that big wooden box could be called a horse. When I looked around everyone was bigger and taller than me, and I felt a little dribble of something come out of my ear. I felt sick and I couldn't eat my meatloaf. I got told off. I had to eat all the leftovers.

That night while I was sleeping my brains leaked all over the sheets. My mother was angry that she had to wash them but she said it wasn't my fault. It is no one's fault. Some of us are just dumber than others. Some of our needs are very special indeed.

SECURITY

After the long day
My father locks the doors
The windows
The blinds on the windows
He locks out the voice of the wind
The question of yesterday

My mother turns off every light
In every room, in every cupboard
She turns off the TV
The red light of the heart flashing
The last star
In this forever foreign sky

And carefully they lie in bed
Listening to the sound
Of growing children

THE TANK

for Victor

I hum and write, I hum under
my breath and keep writing.
A good bit about the goldfish
in the tank at Bats. The tank
sits on one of the Bats booth
tables. There are three fish.
Two look like ordinary goldfish, but the third has really
black rings on its eyes, like
it's been bashed by the others.
And Victor remarks: *Heidi says
if you tap the tank like this,
you could give them a heart
attack*. And he taps the tank.
And I guess that's what it is
we can feel sometimes,
it's Victor's big fat finger
tapping the tank.

ODE TO THE WAIHI BEACH DUMP

With last year's Hawaiian shirts and derelict prams
we stand

at the comprehensive summer
of your gate

as the hours
shorten and lengthen, hinged

to a broken fence, tethered
to an old fridge.

And so it is
for you,

Waihi Beach Dump, we have travelled the length of
the island to behold your robust offices

which stand like customs houses
on the tip of some

marvellous continent or state –
to greet your custodian

on his constantly changing assortment of chairs,
grander than any border guard

or ambassador. Oh Waihi Beach Dump,
first official museum

of the Twentieth Century, where all cultures are
this moment seamlessly merging,

where the cacti considered dead
on our windowsill

for three successive seasons
now flower and bristle

and move about. Because, regardless of us, life goes on
but never, as it were, far

from here. And because you allow us
such proximity to ourselves,

where each generation deposits its
spinning things,

incomplete puzzles, epileptic frogs,
all those other

hapless remnants of the summer
before last:

'The Anatomy Lesson of Dr Tulp'
in 635 pieces

of which, at least, the surgeon's left eye
and five essential tracts

of background are absent.
Less mourned, the leopardskin

lampshade, MacMonster mask or
McAloon's All-Seeing Eye,

last season's dust crop and the whorls of cabbage
which at last blow free

to Waihi Beach or Athenree. In your expansive architecture
of busted surfboards

and up-ended sofas, a wooden Titanic on
tricycle wheels

rattles towards a half-buried
ice-box.

World without end, and from which, like
these dipping and diving

gulls, we are replenished —
here too

the foundations of a new world, a heavenly city
might be laid.

But you, also, have your limitations, like
NO LATE NITE SHOPPIN'

and in places you are made
of sterner stuff:

the buckled birdcage from which
the entire contents of summer

seem to have flown. Or the missing
sunglasses,

wedding ring or keys to the caravan.
For you, Waihi Beach Dump,

we have navigated a course between islands
of kettles and typewriters,

crossed oceans of dust and gulls and the flattened
bodies of blue cars, to conduct

the mute orchestra which is both you
and ourselves — then stood watching as

a broken, stringless kite
is lifted

from a mound of dead appliances
and borne graciously

towards Mayor Island.
So we move

beyond your walled city and out into
the future

you so eloquently describe for us,
we your ambassadors and each

your sole supplier, counting ourselves
among the wreckers and ruiners,

the cranks and demolition crews who build
and rebuild you. For it is us,

poor souls, who have made you
so rich.

Goldwood Orchard, Waihi, January 2000

LETTER TO FRIENDS FROM DALEY'S FLAT HUT: WALKING THE REES AND THE DART

    Shouldered a great sadness on our backs
    and walked into the wild.
    Found a stone for you,
    fool's silver beside Snowy River,
    and sure like fools
    left it at a hut, on a bunk bed,
    beside the posters that say *piwakawaka, whio, takahe,*
    where the windows are dusted black and gold
    by the dusk and early lamplight,
    like Hotere's Carey's Bay.

        (some stone tried to sit heavy in the mind)
    Twilight, when travellers gather
    boil up billies, unwrap yarns
    to mark their paths back out:
    kea time.

    Underwings red as sundown,
    they arrived as the sky cooled,
    darted about Dart Hut
    mimicked sorrowful, hungry cries –
    which Yuki, a language student, missed
    as she listened to her walkman cassette:
    Birds of New Zealand, sea-bird side.
    Fabio, an Italian, stole out, fed them scroggin;
    they scorned the food for someone's socks,
    tossed and tore them in the alpine tussock.

(some stone rolled away, made the sound of laughter)
Each night, Fabio read a novel in translation:
Faulks' *Birdsong*, pages turned to the window
to catch the last of the light.
We coaxed him over with candles, coffee, oranges:
Santo cielo!
He fenced both hands around the fruit
as if its colour guttered.
Told us of his great-grandfather
gunned down in World War One,
grandparents in camps in World War Two,
and a grandmother who recalled New Zealanders:
young soldiers who freed her village,
gave out oranges from their trucks:
Frutti da bonta, Frutti di pace.

Fabio asked for a photo:
we posed the exchange of an orange.
'*The golden handshakes*?' he tried,
pleased to joke in English.

That night, in his sleep
he shook and cried out
on three high notes
then fell silent.

On the track, near dawn, we almost talked
of what we'd been walking from.
Fabio, a geography student,
came away to study 'of deeper things.
New Zealand my book in the real world.'

I wrote to say
I had a silver stone for you from Snowy River.
It had the weight of a face bent to both hands.
The weight of a future past and lost.
Now it has
the size of a trouble halved.
Light as the heft of paper.
The weight of a bird taken flight.

TWO WORD POEM

The toad sat on a red stool
it was a toadstool.

The rain tied a bow
in the cloud's hair
it was a rainbow.

Which witch put sand
in my sandwich?

I stood under the bridge,
then I understood.

I sat on the ledge and
thought about what I know.
It was knowledge.

FONTANELLO

Now you have closed your fontanelle,
my son, my fontanello, I only know

you through the words that serve
thought with sound and saliva

away from the peachy smell
that never meant anything to me

but presence. Your presence,
little present, fontanello, at my skin.

Oh fontanello, let me in.
Your words are little chinks

through to you, and little bricks
that wall me out. Whisper and shout,

you'll go further than this, I'm reeling you out,
and letting you in, always, fontanello,

ready, once more, to begin.
Look at you, so tall and thin.

THE QUIET PLACE

I cannot set a colour against it
or rest it on my knee.
The sound of a glove pulled on a hand,
amber, through a glass, through a tapestry,
the quiet place opens like water.
As I look into greyness, as the children
look under the stones for the light,
as the tongue of the bells mid-week
calls to a ship or a wedding.
The quiet place.
After the song ends,
after the chemistry – a cooling sky.
As if I were listening to miles
slowly. It's where I outstay my time,
the small boat tied,
the mother ship anchored in the bay.

DOG'S BODY

If this were child's play
and I could choose

I'd be the dog —
body a soft black curve

on the stone flags
of the square outside the gallery —

patient in my red collar
and tongue

all my love
in waiting.

WILD DOGS UNDER MY SKIRT

I want to tattoo my legs.
Not blue or green
but black.

I want to sit opposite the tufuga
and know he means me pain.
I want him to bring out his chisel
and hammer
and strike my thighs
the whole circumference of them
like walking right round the world
like paddling across the whole Pacific
in a log
knowing that once you've pushed off
loaded the dogs on board
there's no looking back now, Bingo.

I want my legs as sharp as dogs' teeth
wild dogs
wild Samoan dogs
the mangy kind that bite strangers.

I want my legs like octopus
black octopus
that catch rats and eat them.

I even want my legs like centipedes
the black ones
that sting and swell for weeks.

And when it's done
I want the tufuga
to sit back and know they're not his
they never were

I want to frighten my lovers
let them sit across from me
and whistle through their teeth.

COMMUNION

There will be tea in a mug.

I will make it on the table in front of him. We will talk about high blood pressure and how the fish are biting. He will discuss the changes to dairy farming during the period 1945-1975 and how they have impacted heavily on the rural sector. He will forget the sugar then tell me it could eventually kill me.

There will be tea in a cup.

The cup will have roses on it. The sugar will be well stirred. A small measure of tea will spill onto the saucer which matches the cup it usually rests beneath in the glass-panelled cabinet beside the piano. We will talk about cats and strokes and getting old.

He will talk about Aucklanders and his 'prostrate.'

Both annoy him. I will be offered a beer which will be refused apologetically before I have answered. Tea will eventually come in a pot with a silver spout. He will have to excuse himself as it is poured.

She will provide bacon, eggs, sausages and chips with scones and raspberry jam.

I will be given a glass of Fanta because I am a boy. We will talk about high cholesterol, ischaemic heart disease and recent blood tests. She will tell me it is marvellous what my tests can tell.

I will tell her three things remain:

Aspirin,
Surgery,
And a cup of tea,

but the greatest of these
is a cup of tea.

THE STRONG MOTHERS

Where are the mothers who held power
and children, preserved peaches
in season, understood about
greens and two classes of protein
who drove cars or did not have a licence
who laughed, raged and were there?
Take Mrs Russell who rode her irate bike,
an upright fly that buzzed
with a small engine on its back wheel
up South Road past the school football field
on her way to the hospital. Consider
the other Mrs Russell, drama judge, teacher of
speech and elocution in a small front room,
part-time reporter on *The Hawera Star*.
And Mrs Ellingham who had an MA in French,
ah, the university. Or Mrs Smith, one knee stiff
with TB, her tennis parties on Saturdays, adults
on banks and we smoked their cigarettes in the bamboo.
Her legs shone, their skin in diamonds like a lizard's.
Then Mrs Chapman who sang in the church choir,
formed brooches from fresh white bread,
made you look for a needle till you found it,
heated records and shaped them into vases for presents
who did a spring display in the window of Gamages Hats.

They have left the vowels uncorrected, the stories unproofed.
They have rested their bicycles inside their garages,
looked up the last word, la dernière mot, in Harraps Dictionary,

let needles lie in the narrow dust between verandah boards.
They have tested the last jam on a saucer by the window
comforted the last crying child they will ever see,
and left. How we miss them and their great strength.
Wait for us, we say, wait for me.
And they will.

I COME FROM PALMERSTON NORTH

The fact of the matter is
I was born at Palmerston North Public Hospital
at 12.40 a.m. on the first of April, 1966.

My father, Timothy John Brown, tried to get the date
put back to March 31st
in order to claim a full year's tax rebate
from the government.

The following year the Beatles released *Sgt. Pepper's*
and the Velvet Underground released *The Velvet Underground & Nico*.
My initials – JSB – are the same as Johann Sebastian Bach's.

My father and mother are not originally from Palmerston North.
They immigrated there from across the world and never left,
even though they managed to leave each other.

The Palmerston North Boys' High School yearbook is called
The Palmerstonian. But I do not think of myself as a Palmerstonian.
People from Gore do not think of themselves as Gorons.
I come from Palmerston North.

While still attending PNBHS, schoolboy Craig Wickes played 14 minutes
for the All Blacks against Fiji in 1980. Imagine
the town's pride and anxiety as, ball in hand,
he ran at his opposite number and bounced
out of contention.

He once threw mud at my friend Robert Rieger.
Robert is the son of Paul Rieger – a long-time Mayor of Palmerston North.

Robert also went on to become very successful
— as a Catholic priest.

1994 was the year Palmerston North changed its subtitle from
Rose City to Knowledge City. I do not know if Mayor Rieger
was responsible for this or not.

Palmerston North sports a teachers college and a university, plus
the Universal College of Learning, the International Pacific College *and*
the Adidas Institute of Rugby.
Knowledge City probably wasn't any one person's idea.

Palmerston North is the spiritual home of stockcar racing in New Zealand.
The local team, the Palmerston North Panthers, have won 9 of the 21 titles
since Team Champs were introduced in 1981.

Lots of famous people come from Palmerston North.
Alan Gregg, bass player with popular band the Mutton Birds,
was once asked if he had roots in jazz. He replied
that he had roots in Palmerston North.

I have often wanted to use that joke myself,
and last week I got the opportunity when someone asked me
where I thought I was coming from.

I come from Palmerston North. We are a modest people,
but we are fiercely proud of the bustling, go-ahead city
at the heart of the Manawatu Plains.

In sci-fi movies, people often go back in time in order to try
and change history. This is impossible. You cannot change the past.
And nobody from Palmerston North
would want to.

DOCUMENTARIES

I have seen many documentaries about sex.
Hollywood Sex. British Sex.

Foreign sex
translated into English.

They feature chocolate willy factories
that never ran with the idea of clitoris allsorts.

A woman on the street admits
she came to masturbation late in life

a young man – four times a day, he says,
if I haven't got a girlfriend.

Some men smear themselves with food,
they call it splooshing and say

when you crack an egg on your chest
there's that moment of suspense.

Sissy boys and adult babies
aren't paedophiles.

When I get home from work, says the lorry driver,
I put my nappies on straight away.

My mother died when I was young
so I never had any love you know.

It's a good thing we have documentaries
isn't it, to keep us up to date

keep us well informed
about the issues of the day.

No wonder clever people say –
well I hardly ever watch TV

just the news, oh,
and I like a good documentary.

1YA

you get the radio on
& hear the bird of the day
which sounds like any other
whistle being fed into the 9
o'clock beeps with news

*

you know wellington is there *somewhere*
forming some sort of front.

*

there is a red light on the transistor
you got from the dick smith store

*

you are connected
by a tuner

*

from the volume you will come to know
all those people going about
their steps   up   up
into their warm lives
to stay put from the wind
which is for sure a *hurtler*.

*

you will come to believe
that wellington lies inside a radio
& bleak is on a m

*

there will be much talk about
who the weather is heading for
& how wellington is forgot
of the sun.
*

& you will remember vic's uncle pat
of petone
& the smell of his hands
in the wet flatette
& how his loose phlegm cough
broke free of itself
on the carpet by your feet
*

you can turn wellington
off with your thumb.
*

NOWHERE

By the side of the road
You unfold your flat earth
And consult it for directions.

Little round towns are threaded
Yellow on a red road
Winding round the numbered
mountains.

But here, there is no
Golf course
Rest area
Scenic view
Historic place
Or motor camp:

Look up. Perfect summer blue
Shows between the leaves
Of a spreading puriri
Old as the hills.

Look down. Through the dry grass
The black ants crackle.
They've found your biscuits.

According to the AA
You are nowhere.

Now you know.

notes

1: This poem of landfall appears, untitled, in A.S. Thomson's *The Story of New Zealand* (London, 1859). Thomson writes: 'The Hawaiki fleet reached New Zealand when the pohutukaua [sic] and rata trees were covered with blossoms. It was consequently summer, and the emigrants, like the survivors of a wreck, scattered themselves over the country. To appease the spirit of the land for their intrusion humiliating prayers were said; one uttered by a chief on this celebrated occasion is still preserved as a modern charm.'

2: Cilla McQueen (b. 1949) has always lived in or near Dunedin; she currently lives in Bluff, where she writes full time. 'Living Here' is from her first poetry collection, *Homing In* (1982) which – like two of her subsequent books, *Benzina* (1988) and *Berlin Diary* (1990) – won the New Zealand Book Award for Poetry. *Axis: Poems and Drawings* (2001) is a selection of her work until 1993. More recent poems and drawings are collected in *Markings* (2000) and *Soundings* (2002).

3: A Maori waiata translated by Edward Shortland (1812–1893). A considerable scholar and linguist, Shortland travelled extensively on foot in the South Island in 1843–1844. He published several books, including *Traditions and Superstitions of the New Zealanders* (London, 1854) which contains this poem. Shortland titles his English translation 'Ode', and comments in a footnote: 'This song was composed by a young woman forsaken by her lover.'

4: Chris Orsman (b. 1955) trained as an architect and worked for some time as an ambulance officer before becoming an architectural historian. He lives in Wellington, where he is now a full-time writer. 'Ghost Ships' appeared in the prize-winning *Ornamental Gorse* (1994). *South* (1996) retells the tragic South Polar expedition of Robert Falcon Scott. *Black South* (1998) further elaborates this Antarctic material.

5: Anonymous song collected in the United States of America, ostensibly written by David Lowriston who along with his gang of ten sealers was set down on an island off the South Island's West Coast in February 1810. The men survived nearly four years and had acquired 14,000 sealskins before being picked up by the *Governor Bligh*. See Rona Bailey and Herbert Roth, *Shanties by the Way: A Selection of New Zealand Popular Songs and Ballads* (1967).

6: This whimsical blend of geography and married love is from Horace Fildes's manuscript notebook, *Fugitive Verse of Early New Zealand*, which is held in the Beaglehole Room at Victoria University Library. Fildes seems to have found the poem in *The United Service Journal* (March 1836). 'These lines,' he writes, 'have so far the merit of truth and reality, that they were actually, as they profess to have been, written at the Antipodes, apparently by an English naval officer.'

7: Perhaps the only poem by James Edward Fitzgerald (1818–1896), the first superintendent of Canterbury province. Fitzgerald emigrated to New Zealand on the *Charlotte Jane*, which anchored in Lyttelton Harbour on December 16, 1850. The poem appears in O.T.J. Alpers's *The Jubilee Book of Canterbury Rhymes* (1900); Alpers seems to suggest that it was written at sea on November 1, 1850.

8: John Barr (1809–1889) emigrated to New Zealand from Scotland and farmed for several years at a property he named Craigielee before settling in Dunedin. He was one of the founders of the Burns Society and was well known for his poetry recitals. In his preface to *Poems and Songs*,

Descriptive and Satirical (Edinburgh, 1861), he says that many of his poems 'were composed when the author was busily employed upon his ground, clearing with his axe, and many a long and sad thought did they help to beguile both by night and by day; the writing of them out being, for a considerable time, his greatest recreation after his day's labour.' 'Weans': young children; 'bauchles': old, worn-out shoes; 'roupit to the door': sold up and evicted.

9: This poem by Fiona Farrell (b. 1947) is from *Passengers*, a performance work dealing with the experiences of young working-class women migrants. Charlotte O'Neil was a seventeen-year-old who emigrated to New Zealand as a 'general servant' on the *Isabella Hercus*. Farrell, an award-winning author, has published two books of poems: *Cutting Out* (as Fiona Farrell Poole; 1987) and *The Inhabited Initial* (1999). *Cutting Out* includes songs from the *Passengers* sequence. There are two collections of short stories and several well-regarded novels – most recently *Book Book* (2004), which is a fictional memoir. Farrell has also worked as a playwright and theatre director.

10: Ruth Dallas is the pen-name of Ruth Mumford. She was born in Invercargill in 1919 and published her first verse collection, *Country Road and Other Poems, 1947–52*, with the Caxton Press in 1953. She has published several volumes of poetry since then, including *Collected Poems* and a volume of short fiction, *The Black Horse and other stories* (both 2000). As well as poetry, she has written several books for children. An autobiography, *Curved Horizon*, was published in 1991. 'Pioneer Woman with Ferrets' is from Dallas's 1976 collection, *Walking on the Snow*.

11: Jessie Mackay (1864–1938) included 'The Charge at Parihaka' in her first book of poems, *The Spirit of the Rangatira and Other Ballads* (Melbourne, 1889), which was published when she was 25. The poem parodies 'The Charge of the Light Brigade', Tennyson's famous panegyric about doomed courage against impossible odds, and mocks the excessive caution shown when in November 1881 large numbers of European troops marched on Parihaka to arrest Te Whiti and Tohu. They met no resistance. As Jessie Mackay observes in a note, 'the campaign terminated without a scratch. The affair caused some real apprehension in the North Island, and a good deal of burlesque sentiment in the South.' A range of poems about Parihaka by recent New Zealand poets can be found in *Parihaka: The Art of Passive Resistance* (2001).

12: W.H. Oliver (b. 1925) has published three substantial books of poetry. 'Parihaka' is from his second collection, *Out of Season* (1980). A noted historian, Oliver was for many years Professor of History at Massey University and the founding editor of *The Dictionary of New Zealand Biography*. His books include *The Story of New Zealand* (1960), *James K. Baxter: A Portrait* (1983), and – as editor – *The Oxford History of New Zealand* (1981). More recently there is a memoir, *Looking for the Phoenix* (2002).

13: Arthur H. Adams (1872–1936) was born in Lawrence, attended the University of Otago and, after travelling in China and England, settled in Sydney where he worked as literary editor on the *Bulletin* and also edited the Sydney *Sun*. His published work includes several novels and plays. 'The Dwellings of our Dead' appears in his first verse collection *Maoriland and Other Verses* (Sydney, 1899).

14: David McKee Wright (1869–1928) was born in Ireland and came to New Zealand in 1887. For several years he worked as a farmhand and rabbiter on Otago stations, where he began writing poetry, especially ballads about local life and identities. His books included *Aorangi and Other Verses* (Dunedin, 1896), *Station Ballads and Other Verses* (Dunedin, 1897) and *New Zealand Chimes* (Wellington, 1900). 'His themes are homely,' wrote Rutherford Waddell in an introduction to *Station Ballads*, 'but that is what we most need.' McKee Wright moved to Sydney in 1909, succeeding Arthur H. Adams as literary editor of the *Bulletin*. His pen names as a working journalist included Pat o' Maori, Curse o' Moses and Mary Commonwealth.

15: Dinah Hawken was born in Hawera in 1943. For many years she worked as a student counsellor; she now writes full time and teaches a small workshop, 'Writing the Landscape', at Victoria University. Her first collection of poetry, *It Has No Sound and is Blue*, won the Commonwealth Poetry Prize for Best First Book in 1987. 'The Tug of War' is a short section from her book-length poetry sequence *Small Stories of Devotion* (1991). A volume of selected and new work, *Oh There You Are Tui!*, was published in 2001.
See http://www.nzepc.auckland.ac.nz/authors/hawken/

16: Thomas Bracken (1843–1898) was born in Ireland and came to New Zealand in 1869. Probably New Zealand's most popular 19th-century poet, he published several books of verse, including *Lays of the Land of the Maori and Moa* (London, 1884) and *Musings in Maoriland* (Dunedin, 1890). A century after his death, he is remembered as the author of 'God Defend New Zealand', but for many years he was best known for 'Not Understood', a poem that many New Zealanders once knew by heart. In the front of the fifth (pocket) edition of *Not Understood and Other Poems* (Wellington, 1909), mention is made of the professional verse reciter, Mel. B. Spurr, who 'enumerating some of his most successful recitations ... came "finally" to "Not Understood" – "that charming little bit of philosophy by the late Thomas Bracken, which I now give almost every evening. I am hoping to introduce it to an English public some time next year, and I predict for it an instantaneous and unprecedented success."'

17: Peter Bland (b. 1934) came to New Zealand from Yorkshire in 1954, and published his first collection of poems in 1958. His volume of *Selected Poems* was published in 1987. Recent books include *Let's Meet: Poems 1985–2003* and *Ports of Call*, both published in 2003. As well as writing poetry, Peter Bland has worked as a playwright and actor both in New Zealand and in the United Kingdom. His 2004 memoir, *Sorry, I'm a Stranger Here Myself*, includes a selection of poems written between 1958 and 1965. Farmer and naturalist W.H. Guthrie-Smith (1861–1940) was born in Scotland and emigrated to New Zealand in 1880. His book *Tutira* (1921), a classic of New Zealand literature, is a detailed study of all aspects of his Hawke's Bay sheep station of the same name.

18: Anne Glenny Wilson, neé Adams (1848–1930) was born in Victoria and came to New Zealand in 1874 when she married James (later Sir James) Wilson, a wealthy farmer and member of Parliament. She published novels as well as poetry, often under the pen name 'Austral' or as Mrs James Glenny Wilson. 'A Spring Afternoon in New Zealand' was published in *Themes and Variations* (London, 1889). A reviewer in Edinburgh's *Scotsman* said, 'If the Great Britain of the South has not already chosen a Laureate, it will not fare ill by placing the circlet of leaves on the head of "Austral"', while Sir Robert Stout wrote that 'in the after years [*Themes and Variations*] will be recognised as one of the first volumes of verse written by one who was born under the Southern Cross, that shows that we have at last in the Southern land a literature of our own.'

19: William Charles Hodgson (1826–1894) came to New Zealand at the age of seventeen. In 1863 he became Inspector of Schools in Nelson, a territory that then included Marlborough and the West Coast. *Poems of William Hodgson* was published posthumously in 1896, edited and introduced by Alfred A. Grace. Hodgson's poems are mostly dated imitations of classical models, very comfortable with words like vale, brook and grove. 'The Lay of the Weather-Bound', is one of the poet's far livelier 'Nelson Lays', where, as Alfred Grace writes, he has 'abandoned his high classical standards for more modern ones. [The lays] are included in this collection chiefly on account of a local interest attaching to them.'

20: William Satchell (1860–1942) was born in London and came to New Zealand in 1886. He published four novels, but no verse collections. 'Song of the Gumfield' appears in his first novel,

The Land of the Lost (London, 1902), but it first appeared in the *Bulletin* in 1896 under the pen name Saml. Cliall White, an anagram of the author's name.

21: Blanche (B.E.) Baughan (1870–1958) was born in London and published two collections of verse before coming to New Zealand in 1900. Her New Zealand collections are *Shingle-Short and Other Verses* (1908) and *Poems from the Port Hills* (1923), though she wrote little poetry after 1910. She worked for prison reform and was Akaroa's first woman councillor. Baughan wrote many booklets describing New Zealand's scenery; the phrase, 'The Finest Walk in the World', was first used as a title for her article on the Milford Track, originally printed in London's *Spectator*.

22: 'The Windy Hills o' Wellington' appeared in *The New Zealand Times* on 27 January, 1894, where it is attributed to 'The Exile'. It is usually assumed that 'The Exile' was the Australian ballad and story writer Henry Lawson (1867–1922), who was in New Zealand at the time.

23: The first book of poems by Kevin Ireland (b. 1933), *Face to Face*, was published in 1963 and his *Selected Poems* (which includes 'The First Tribute' among its 'new poems') in 1987. Ireland has worked as a magazine and newspaper sub-editor both in London and in Auckland, where he now lives. As well as poetry collections, he has published novels and two volumes of autobiography, the first of which – *Under the Bridge and Over the Moon* (1999) – won a Montana New Zealand Book Award. Matthew McKinney was Ireland's great-uncle.

24: From Lloyd Jones's *The Book of Fame* (2000), the award-winning novel that recreates the story of the 1905 tour of Great Britain by the All Black rugby team known as 'The Originals'. The novel is written in the third-person plural (as if the voice of the team, and sometimes even a nation, is speaking), while the author's prose is often close to free verse and his paragraphs to stanzas. The extract comes from the chapter titled 'How We Think', where the team visits the universities of Oxford and Cambridge. Lloyd Jones (b. 1955) has mostly written novels (among them *Choo Woo* and *Here at the End of the World We Learn to Dance*); but there is also a book of short stories and a controversial travel book, *Biografi* (1993), which blends fact and fiction.

25: Arnold Wall (1869–1966) was born in England and came to Canterbury as Professor of English in 1898. He led a rich and busy life as a teacher, writer, broadcaster, botanist and mountain climber. 'The City from the Hills' was first published in his collection *Blank Verse Lyrics and Other Poems* 'by a Colonial Professor'(London, 1900). The city itself is Christchurch.

26: John Gallas was born in Wellington in 1950, but has lived in England since 1971. He has published several books of poetry in the United Kingdom and is author/editor/translator of *The Song Atlas*, 'the world's first anthology of poetry from every country in the world'. 'Anzac Snap' is from his most recent poetry collection, *Star City* (Carcanet Press, 2004). See www.johngallaspoetry.co.uk

27: Katherine Mansfield (pen name of Kathleen Beauchamp, 1888–1923). 'L.H.B.' was Mansfield's only brother, Leslie ('Chummie'), who was killed by a faulty hand-grenade in the First World War in October 1915. A friend told Mansfield that his last words were, 'Lift my head, Katy, I can't breathe.' In a letter from Bandol to John Middleton Murry (16 December, 1915), she wrote: 'Since I have been alone here the loss of my little brother has become quite real to me. I have entered into my loss if you know what I mean – Always before that I shrank from the final moment – but now it is past.' Mansfield's poems are most easily read in *The Poems of Katherine Mansfield*, edited by Vincent O'Sullivan (1988).

28: Ursula Bethell (1874–1945) was born in England, grew up in New Zealand, then spent her twenties and thirties in Britain and Europe before returning to live in Christchurch. Her first book of poetry was published in 1929 under the pseudonym Evelyn Hayes. Its title, *From A Garden in the Antipodes*, indicates the kind of work the volume contained: poems (such as

'Response') recording the temporal rhythms of Bethell's Cashmere garden, often written with English friends in mind and sometimes sent abroad in letters. A volume of Bethell's *Collected Poems*, edited by Vincent O'Sullivan, was published in 1997. An edition of her letters, edited by Peter Whiteford, is also planned. See http://www.nzepc.auckland.ac.nz/authors/bethell

29: R.A.K. Mason (1905–1971) was born in Auckland, of New Zealand-born parents. His book *The Beggar*, which contains 'Old Memories of Earth', was published in 1924. The early readership for Mason's work was not large; he is said to have thrown about 200 unsold copies of *The Beggar* – nine-tenths of the edition – off Auckland's Queens Wharf. Nevertheless Allen Curnow has judged Mason 'his country's first wholly original, unmistakably gifted poet.' Mason wrote little poetry of note after the 1930s. His *Collected Poems* was published in 1990 and an award-winning biography by Rachel Barrowman in 2003.

30: Eileen Duggan (1894–1972) was a brilliant classical scholar and a devout Roman Catholic. Her poems – mostly Georgian in manner – were published in book form in Britain and the United States as well as in New Zealand. Her reputation was at its height in the thirties and forties, but has fluctuated since. 'The Bushfeller' appeared in *Poems*, published in London in 1937 with an introduction by Walter de la Mare.

31: 'Trees' is by Una Currie, and appears in the much-maligned 1930 anthology *Kowhai Gold*, along with five other poems by the same author. Currie does not seem to have published any individual volumes of verse.

32: Denis Glover (1912–1980) was a notable printer as well as a poet. He founded the Caxton Press, which published many important books of New Zealand poetry. His own poetry is lyrical and satirical by turns. 'The Magpies', with its Depression landscape, is probably the nearest thing New Zealand verse has to a 'classic' (though Glover's own *Sings Harry* sequence would run it close); it first appeared in *Recent Poems* (1941). The 1996 *Selected Poems* edited by Bill Manhire is the most convenient introduction to his work. A biography of Glover, by Gordon Ogilvie, was published in 1999.

33: A.R.D. Fairburn (1904–1957) included this poem in his 1946 volume, *The Rakehelly Man*, and like Glover's 'The Magpies' it seems to articulate Depression experiences. Fairburn, whose great-grandfather came to New Zealand as a missionary in 1819, was born in Auckland, and became well known as a poet and lively polemicist. Despite two biographies (one by James and Helen McNeish, the other by Denys Trussell) and the 2004 collection of short reminiscences *Fairburn and Friends*, his reputation as a poet has waned over the years. The poems are now most easily found in the *Selected Poems* edited by Mac Jackson in 1995.
See http://www.nzepc.auckland.ac.nz/authors/fairburn/

34: Bub Bridger (b. 1924) is an extremely popular performance poet who didn't begin writing until she was sixty. She is of mixed Irish and Maori ancestry, and 'Johnny Come Dancing' is dedicated to her Irish father. The word 'Douglas' in the poem's first line is pronounced 'Dooglies'. Bub Bridger's one book of poems, *Up Here on the Hill*, was published in 1989.

35: Charles Brasch (1909–1973) has been an influential figure in New Zealand writing, especially through his work as founding editor of the literary magazine *Landfall*. There is a posthumous *Collected Poems* edited by Alan Roddick (1984), and an autobiographical work, *Indirections: A Memoir*, was published in 1980. Donald Kerr has edited a collection of essays, *Enduring Legacy: Charles Brasch, Poet, Patron & Collector* (2003). 'The Islands' is printed here as it first appeared in *Disputed Ground, Poems 1939–45* (1948); the *Collected Poems* gives Brasch's later revision.

36: J. R. Hervey (1889–1958) was born in Southland and ordained as an Anglican priest. He published four volumes of poetry with the Caxton Press between 1940 and 1955. 'She Was My

Love Who Could Deliver' is from *She Was My Spring* (1955), a book dedicated 'In Praise, Gratitude and Humility . . . to the dear memory of Ethel, my wife.'

37: Robin Hyde (pen name of Iris Guiver Wilkinson, 1906–1939) was a most prolific writer: a novelist and hard-working journalist as well as a poet. Much of her fiction is still in print, and a collection of her non-fiction prose, *Disputed Ground: Robin Hyde, Journalist*, edited by Gillian Boddy and Jacqueline Matthews, was published in 1991. *The Book of Iris*, a biography by Hyde's son Derek Challis, and *Young Knowledge: The Poems of Robin Hyde* (ed. Michele Leggott) have subsequently been published (in 2002 and 2003 respectively). This poem is 'Section VI from The Beaches', which is itself part of the book-length sequence, 'The Houses by the Sea'. See http://www.nzepc.auckland.ac.nz/authors/hyde/

38: Donald McDonald (1912–1942) was, as this poem suggests, a farmer; he died in the Second World War. He was educated at the Agricultural High School in Feilding, which published his poems after his death 'In remembrance of Old Boys fallen in the War and in Memory of the Author, Donald McDonald'. 'Benchy': probably refers to the narrow sheep tracks that terrace hillside paddocks.

39: Janet Frame (1924–2004) had a single collection of poems, *The Pocket Mirror* (1967), published in her lifetime. A volume of unpublished poems is forthcoming. Frame is a poet in all her work – in her novels, autobiographical writings and short stories. 'A Note on the Russian War' appeared in 1951 in her first book, *The Lagoon and Other Stories*, as it is also regarded as a prose work, and is reprinted in her 1983 volume of selected stories, *You Are Now Entering the Human Heart*. In 2004, *The Lagoon* and *The Pocket Mirror* were reprinted as a single volume.

40: This poem was published in *New Zealand Farm and Station Verse* (ed. A.E. Woodhouse, 1950), where a note makes it clear that the author, Bruce Stronach, worked for many years as a musterer on South Island sheep stations: 'the dog, Boy, made his "Last Run" on Mt White.'

41: William Hart-Smith (1911–1990) was born in England and came to New Zealand in 1924. He began writing in New Zealand but lived in Australia for extended periods and thought of himself as essentially an Australian poet. His work, however, appears in both Australian and New Zealand verse anthologies. 'Subject Matter' first appeared in *Landfall* in 1949. The fullest selection of Hart-Smith's poems is *Hand to Hand: A Garnering*, edited by Barbara Petrie and published in Australia in 1991; this book also contains essays on the poet's life and work.

42: Mary Stanley (1919–1980) was a graduate of the University of Auckland; she worked as a teacher. Her one book of poems, *Starveling Year*, was published by Pegasus in 1953. Stanley was married to the poet Kendrick Smithyman, who edited the posthumous *Starveling Year and Other Poems* (1994). See http://www.nzepc.auckland.ac.nz/authors/stanley/

43: Rachel McAlpine (b. 1940) is indeed one of six girls, the subject of 'Before the Fall' and – as the poem suggests – her father was an Anglican clergyman. McAlpine is known for her plays and novels as well as for her poetry. Her first books were collections of poems; her *Selected Poems* was published in 1988. She has also edited *Another 100 New Zealand Poems for Children* (2001) and produced several non-fiction books.

44: Peter Cape (1926–1979) worked in film, radio and television for some years, and later as a full-time freelance writer concentrating on New Zealand arts and crafts. He remains well known for his songs, of which 'Taumarunui' and 'Down the Hall on Saturday Night' are probably the most popular. The texts of his songs and a brief autobiography were published as *Ordinary Joker* (2001).

45: This song appears in Joe Charles's *Black Billy Tea: New Zealand Ballads* (Christchurch, 1981). Charles writes there: 'In the shearing shed at "Farfield" in the Glenroy district, where we had a farm in the 1950s, I was asked by my neighbour, Doug Gray, to put on the billy for the shearers' morning smoko. Ray Pareka, the "gun" shearer, knowing my kind of brew from the days of building bridges for the Selwyn County Council, said, "No dish-water, Joe – I like it *black*!" Black billy tea! To the beat of the old petrol engine driving the machines I strung it all together. . . . Les Cleveland set it to music and it became my first recorded song.'

46: Hone Tuwhare (b. 1922) belongs to the Ngapuhi hapu Ngati Korokoro, Ngati Tautahi and Te Popoto. His first (and frequently reprinted) book of poems, *No Ordinary Sun*, appeared in 1964. There have been many volumes since then, including an updated collected poems, *Deep River Talk*. Janet Hunt's *Hone Tuwhare* (1998) is both a biography and an anthology of important poems. Hone Tuwhare has received many awards and honours, including a Montana New Zealand Book Award for *Piggy-back Moon* (2001), which collects poems from his term as Te Mata Estate New Zealand Poet Laureate. A full-time writer for many years, he originally trained and worked as a boilermaker. 'Monologue' first appeared in *No Ordinary Sun*.

47: M.K. Joseph (1914–1981) is probably better known for his novels (and their remarkable variety) than for his poetry. He was born in London and came to New Zealand in 1924; he taught for many years in the Department of English at the University of Auckland. 'Secular Litany' first appeared in *Imaginary Worlds* (1950) and was anthologised occasionally in the fifties and sixties, though Joseph did not include it in *Inscription on a Paper Dart: Selected Poems 1945–72* (1974).

48: 'Telephone Wires' was written by a twelve-year-old schoolgirl, Mary, in the mid-1950s. The poem was printed in Elwyn Richardson's book *In the Early World* (1964). Richardson taught at the small school of Oruaiti in Northland, and in his book he records and writes about the remarkable work – not only in poetry but also in the visual arts – that his pupils produced.

49: Keith Sinclair (1922–1993) was a notable historian, for many years Professor of History at Auckland University, and the author of a number of important books including the Penguin *A History of New Zealand* (first published in 1959 and rarely out of print) and a biography of Walter Nash. Some of his best-known poems, too, explored historical themes. His first collection of verse appeared in 1952; *Moontalk: Poems New and Selected* was published in 1993.

50: Louis Johnson (1924–1988) worked as a journalist, teacher and editor. He was the founding editor of the *New Zealand Poetry Yearbook*, which ran from 1951 until the mid-sixties. His first collection of poetry was published in 1945, and his many other titles include *Bread and a Pension* (1964), *True Confessions of the Last Cannibal* (1986) and the posthumous *Last Poems* (1990). In the fifties and sixties he and other poets such as James K. Baxter deliberately sought to introduce suburban subjects into New Zealand verse. Terry Sturm edited Johnson's *Selected Poems* in 2000.

51: Kendrick Smithyman (1922–1995) taught for many years in the English Department at the University of Auckland. He was a particularly prolific poet, with publications including the book-length poem *Atua Wera* (1997). His collected poems are progressively being published on-line at http://www.smithymanonline.auckland.ac.nz. There are some 1500 individual poems, selected by the author before his death; over one third are available for the first time. Smithyman's critical study of New Zealand poetry, *A Way of Saying*, was published in 1965. See http://www.nzepc.auckland.ac.nz/authors/smithyman/

52: Fleur Adcock was born in Auckland in 1934 but spent much of her childhood, including the years of the Second World War, in England. She studied Classics at Victoria University of Wellington before travelling in 1963 to London, where she worked as a librarian. Though she has remained in Britain and been a full-time writer there since 1977, she regularly visits New Zealand where members of her family (including the five-year-old of this poem) continue to live. 'For a Five-Year-Old' is the final poem in Adcock's first poetry collection, *The Eye of the Hurricane* (1964). Her *Poems 1960–2000* was published in the United Kingdom in 2000.

See http://www.contemporarywriters.com/authors/?p=auth161

53: Vincent O'Sullivan was born in Auckland in 1937; he worked as an academic for a number of years, then as a freelance writer on both sides of the Tasman. Between 1987 and 2004 he was Professor of English at Victoria University. O'Sullivan's *Selected Poems* was published in 1992, but he is equally well known as a short story writer, dramatist, editor and critic. His most recent books of poetry are: *Seeing You Asked* (1998, winner of a Montana New Zealand Book Award), *Lucky Table* (2001) and *Nice Morning for it, Adam* (2004). He has published several works of fiction and a biography of the writer John Mulgan. Rawleigh products still exist, though they are less often sold door to door.

54: Alistair Te Ariki Campbell was born in Rarotonga in 1925, and sent to New Zealand after the deaths of his Scottish father and Polynesian mother. His first poetry collection, *Mine Eyes Dazzle*, was an immediate success when published in 1951. There have been many volumes of poetry since, including *Stone Rain: The Polynesian Strain* (1992) which collects Campbell's verse on Maori and Polynesian themes. His *Pocket Collected Poems* was published in 1996. More recently he has published poetry about Gallipoli and about the Maori Battalion. Among his other writings are a short autobiography, *Island to Island* (1984) and a trilogy of novels that focus on the Pacific. 'Why Don't You Talk to Me?' was first published in *Blue Rain* (1967).

55: 'A Small Ode on Mixed Flatting' was first published in 1967 as a broadsheet response to the prohibition it describes. James K. Baxter (1926–1972) was at the time Burns Fellow at the University of Otago. Baxter's colourful life has been traced in two biographies (by Frank McKay and W.H. Oliver) and his *Collected Poems* (ed. J.E. Weir) was published in 1979. *New Selected Poems* has recently been edited by Baxter scholar Paul Millar. Baxter's views on New Zealand puritanism never wavered, though his poems were not always as straightforwardly satirical or comic as this one; many of the poems written after 1969, when Baxter went to live at Jerusalem on the Wanganui River, are notable for their contemplative qualities. As well as poetry, Baxter wrote stage and radio plays, a short novel and various kinds of non-fiction.

56: David Mitchell (b. 1940) was – like Peter Olds, Sam Hunt, Ian Wedde and others – one of the 'young New Zealand poets' who came to prominence in the sixties and seventies. (The designation comes from the anthology edited by Arthur Baysting in 1973.) 'Th Ballad of Rosy Crochet' is from Mitchell's 1972 collection, *Pipe Dreams in Ponsonby*. Since that book, which was reprinted in 1975, Mitchell has published sparingly, and in recent years not at all.

57: Peter Olds (b. 1944) lives near Dunedin. In 1973, introducing his poems in *The Young New Zealand Poets*, he wrote: '& now, after 16 blood transfusions & 8 hundred gallons of legal chloropromazine I still write poems to submit to psychiatric Statesmen whose critics doubt my sincerity, insanity, Lady Moss's micro-bus travelling chemical road show; who sleep with 1963 grown-up 'boppers; who flush this crap, my crap, carburettors, dirty pistons, Fred's poetry, your notebooks & mine down gold-plated purple-clouded imaginary candlewick bed-spread grots . . . I guess that's where my poems come from.' 'Revisiting V8 Nostalgia' appears in *Lady Moss Revived* (1972). *It Was a Tuesday Morning: Selected Poems 1972–2001* was published in 2004.

58: Sam Hunt (b. 1946), almost certainly New Zealand's best-known poet and a writer of great formal skill, is the nearest thing we have to a troubadour. Many of his poems like this one, first published in the 1975 collection *Time to Ride*, are closely related to song. Hunt spends much of his time touring and performing his work around New Zealand. His *Selected Poems* was published in 1987. Though he prefers to perform his poems rather than see them on the page, he has nevertheless published some seventeen titles over the years.

59: Ian Wedde (b. 1946) is probably the most admired poet of his generation. As the last stanzas of this poem indicate, it was written partly in response to one of the so-called 'Think Big' projects of the Muldoon administration: a proposal to site an aluminium smelter at Aramoana, at the head of Otago Harbour. (Wedde was living in the nearby settlement of Port Chalmers at the time.) The poem was first published in 1975. Wedde's *Driving into the Storm: Selected Poems* was published in 1987; he has written fiction (notably the 1986 novel *Symmes Hole*); and he edited, with Harvey McQueen, *The Penguin Book of New Zealand Verse* (1985), which succeeded Allen Curnow's anthology of the same name. His most recent book of poems is *The Commonplace Odes* (2001), and *How to be Nowhere* (1995) is a collection of critical essays. Wedde works as a freelance writer after some years as an arts project leader at Te Papa.

See http://www.nzepc.auckland.ac.nz/authors/wedde/

60: Florence E. Allan published two slim volumes of verse in the early seventies. *To Land's End and Back* and *Pathway of Memories*. Dates and publishers are not given, but the latter volume where 'What Next?' appears ran to a second edition. Like 'What Next?', her most interesting poems are homely, entertaining anecdotes eked out in curious rhyming couplets.

61: Rore Hapipi (aka Rowley Habib) was born at Oruanui, near Taupo, in 1935. He is of Ngati Tuwharetoa descent through his mother, and of Lebanese descent through his father. He has written short stories as well as poems, and has been actively involved in Maori theatre, particularly through Te Ika a Maui Players and his own play *Death of the Land*. 'Ancestors' was first published in *Landfall* in 1973.

62: Murray Edmond (b. 1949) lives in Auckland and teaches theatre at the University of Auckland. 'Shack' first appeared in *End Wall* (1981). Edmond was a co-founder of the influential poetry magazine *Freed* and, with Alan Brunton and Michele Leggott, he edited *Big Smoke* (2000), an anthology of New Zealand poetry from the sixties and seventies. Recent poetry collections include *Laminations* (2000) and *Fool Moon* (2004).

See http://www.nzepc.auckland.ac.nz/authors/edmond/

63: Michael Jackson (b. 1940) has produced an award-winning book of poems, *Wall* (1980), in which 'Making It Otherwise' is printed. His *Duty Free: Selected Poems, 1965–1988* was published in 1989 and *Antipodes* in 1996. Jackson has worked and taught as an anthropologist, and has mostly lived outside New Zealand: in Sierra Leone, the United States, Australia and – most recently – Denmark. Two interesting prose volumes are *Pieces of Music* (1994) and *At Home in the World* (1995).

64: Wystan Curnow (b. 1939) teaches in the Department of English at Auckland University. Much of his work has appeared in magazines and remains uncollected. This piece is from *Back in the USA: Poems 1980–1982* (1989). Curnow was an editor of the eighties magazine *Splash*, and is well known as an art critic and exhibition curator. Various writings can be read at: http://jackbooks.com/Wystan/Wystan.htm

65: Apirana Taylor (b. 1955) is of Ngati Porou, Te Whanau a Apanui, Taranaki, Ngapuhi and Ngati Pakeha descent. He has been closely involved in the development of Maori theatre. As well as poetry – *Eyes of the Ruru* (1979), *Soft Leaf Falls of the Moon* (1996) – he has published collections of short stories, a novel and two plays. A new collection of poems, *te ata kura: the red-tipped dawn*, has just been published.

66: Throughout his life Allen Curnow (1911–2001) published verse of extraordinary quality. He is still best known in New Zealand for his earlier poems of nationhood ('Landfall in Unknown Seas', 'The Unhistoric Story', 'House and Land' and others), but no single poem will represent the range and integrity of his work, which is best seen in *Early Days Yet: New and Collected Poems 1941–1997*, published in 1997. His last published collection, *The Bells of Saint Babel's*

(2001), won a Montana New Zealand Book Award. 'The Parakeets at Karekare' is from the 1982 collection, *You Will Know When You Get There: Poems 1979–81*. Curnow won the Commonwealth Poetry Prize in 1989, and also received the Queen's Gold Medal for Poetry. As an editor he has been an influential figure, especially through *A Book of New Zealand Verse 1923–45* (1945) and *The Penguin Book of New Zealand Verse* (1960). He also wrote verse plays, and for many years published verse satire under the pen name Whim Wham.

67: Lauris Edmond (1924–2000) only began writing poetry seriously in middle age, a process she describes in the second and third volumes of her autobiography: *Bonfires in the Rain* (1991) and *The Quick World* (1992). Her poems are most readily found in the *Selected Poems* edited by Ken Arvidson (2001); an earlier *Selected Poems* won the 1985 Commonwealth Poetry Prize. Shortly before her death in 2000 she edited the anthology *New Zealand Love Poems*. 'The Names' first appeared in her 1980 collection *Salt From the North*.
See http://www.nzepc.auckland.ac.nz/authors/lauris/

68: Keri Hulme (b. 1947) is of Kai Tahu and Pakeha descent. She is best known as the author of the Booker Prize-winning novel *the bone people*. Other prose works include *Te Kaihau/The Windeater*, *Lost Possessions*, *Homeplaces* (a collaboration with the photographer Robin Morrison) and *Stonefish*, a collection of short fiction (2004). There are two books of poetry, *The Silences Between (Moeraki Conversations)* (1982) and *Strands* (1992), but 'Whakatu' has not been collected. It was first published in the 1982 anthology of writing by Maori, *Into the World of Light*, edited by Witi Ihimaera and Don Long. The poem is based on a children's rhyme; Whakatu is the freezing works near Hastings (it was closed in the mid-eighties, after this poem was written).

69: Iain Sharp was born in Scotland in 1953. He came to New Zealand as a boy, trained and worked as a librarian, but now also earns his living as a freelance writer and newspaper columnist. He produced three short books of poetry in the 1980s: *Why Mammals Shiver* (1980), *She is Trying to Kidnap the Blind Person* (1985) and *The Pierrot Variations* (1985). A selection of his performance poems, *The Singing Harp*, has recently been published. He edited the inaugural issue of the on-line annual *Best New Zealand Poems* at http://www.vuw.ac.nz/modernletters/bnzp/

70: This poem is from *Miracles*, an anthology of poems by children from eighteen English-speaking countries (edited by Richard Lewis, London, 1967). Work by a strikingly large number of New Zealand children appeared in the collection. Glennis Foster was ten when she wrote 'Night and Noises'.

71: John Newton (b. 1959) grew up in a farming district and studied at the Universities of Canterbury and Melbourne. He presently teaches in the Department of English at the University of Canterbury. 'Ferret Trap' is from his book *Tales of the Angler's El Dorado* (1985), a title that echoes the famous travel book by cowboy writer Zane Grey.

72: Hugh Lauder was born in 1938 and educated in England; he came to New Zealand in 1979. In the 1980s he was *Landfall*'s poetry editor, and is now Professor of Education and Political Economy at the University of Bath. 'The Invincible' is from Lauder's 1990 collection, *Knowledge of the Left Hand*, but it refers to 1983 when the British warship the *Invincible* visited Wellington Harbour after the war in the Falklands. Gefn is one of the names of Freyja; she and Odin are Norse gods.

73: West Coast poet Kim Eggleston was born in 1960. She has two published collections of poetry: *From the Face to the Bin* (1984) and *25 Poems* (1985). 'The Back Road Back' is from *25 Poems*.

74: Elizabeth Nannestad (b. 1956) lives near Auckland and has worked in medicine. Her poems have been widely anthologised. Individual collections are *Jump* (1967), which shared the New Zealand Book Award for Poetry with Allen Curnow's *The Loop in Lone Kauri Road*, and *If He's a Good Dog He'll Swim* (1996).

75: Amber McWilliams (b. 1975) has been a professional performer since the age of nine. She starred in Margaret Mahy's *Strangers* and in *The New Adventures of Black Beauty*. This poem was published on the *Sunday Times* children's page when its author was seven.

76: Michael Morrissey (b. 1942) lives in Auckland. He has published several fiction titles (short stories and book-length narratives) as well as books of poetry, and has also edited anthologies of New Zealand short stories. This poem is from his 1986 collection, *Taking in the View*. It refers in passing to T.S. Eliot's famous line about April from *The Waste Land*, to J.D. Salinger's story about suicide, 'A Perfect Day for Bananafish', and to the death of American poet Hart Crane, who jumped from the deck of a ship.

77: Bob Orr (b. 1949) lives in Auckland, where for many years he worked for the Auckland Harbour Board. His books of poetry include *Breeze* (1991) – where 'Thelonious Monk Piano' was collected after its earlier appearance in 1986 in the magazine *Rambling Jack* – and *Valparaiso* (2002). African-American musician Thelonious Monk (1917–1982) was a notable jazz pianist. See http://www.nzepc.auckland.ac.nz/authors/orr/

78: Meg Campbell (b. 1937) lives at Pukerua Bay with her husband Alistair Te Ariki Campbell (see note to poem 54), and runs a small publishing house, Te Kotare Press. Her books are *The Way Back* (1981), *A Durable Fire* (1982), *Orpheus and Other Poems* (1990) and *The Better Part* (2000). 'Viola' is reprinted from *Orpheus and Other Poems*.

79: Owen Marshall (b. 1941) is New Zealand's most admired contemporary short-story writer. He has published many collections of short stories, two novels and a single gathering of poems, *Occasional: 50 Poems* (2004). He has also edited a number of anthologies of New Zealand short stories. 'The Divided World' is the title story of a 1989 volume of selected stories. Something of Marshall's view of poets and poetry can be gathered from another of his stories, 'A Poet's Dream of Amazons', which is most easily read in *The Best of Owen Marshall's Short Stories* (1997).

80: Roma Potiki (Te Aupouri, Te Rarawa, Ngati Rangitihi) was born in 1958 and lives at Paekakariki. As well as writing poetry, she works in theatre, dance and the visual arts. 'Compulsory Class Visits' appears in her collection of poems, *Stones in Her Mouth* (1992). A more recent collection of poetry is *Shaking the Tree* (1998).

81: David Eggleton (b. 1953) is well known as a performance poet; as 'the Mad Kiwi Ranter' he won the British Street Entertainer of the Year Award in 1985. His collections of poetry include *South Pacific Sunrise* (1986), *People of the Land* (1988) and *Rhyming Planet* (2001). 'Postcard' is from *People of the Land*. Recently Eggleton has edited an anthology of New Zealand landscape writing, *Here on Earth* (1999) and has published *Ready to Fly: The Story of New Zealand Rock Music* (2003). He lives in Dunedin, where he works as a full-time writer and reviewer.

82: Michele Leggott (b. 1956) teaches in the Department of English at Auckland University. 'Vanilla Rim' is from *Like This?* (1988), which won the PEN First Book of Poetry Award. Subsequent collections of poems are *Swimmers, Dancers* (1991), the award-winning *DIA* (1994), *As Far as I Can See* (1999, in which she writes about her progressive loss of sight) and *Milk and Honey* (2005). She has published a study of the American poet, Louis Zukofsky, and is a significant Robin Hyde scholar (see note to poem 37). Leggott initiated the New Zealand Electronic Poetry Centre (http://www.nzepc.auckland.ac.nz), where further information about her own work as poet, scholar and critic can be found.

83: Brian Turner (b. 1944) has published eight volumes of poetry, including the award-winning

1992 collection, *Beyond*. 'Chevy' is from his fifth collection, *All that Blue Can Be* (1989). Turner, who lives in Central Otago, has always been associated with Dunedin and southern New Zealand. He has worked as a publisher's editor, but now writes full time, concentrating especially on sports biographies and on environmental issues. His two most recent books of poetry are *Taking Off* (2001) and *Footfall* (2005), which collects poems from his term as Te Mata Estate New Zealand Poet Laureate. There is also a volume of autobiography, *Somebodies and Nobodies* (2002).

84: Geoff Cochrane was born in 1951 and lives in Wellington. This poem first appeared in *Kandinsky's Mirror*, one of several collections that he published in the seventies and eighties. Many poems from these collections appear along with new work in *Aztec Noon* (1992). Subsequent poetry collections are *Into India* (1999), *Acetylene* (2001) and *Vanilla Wine* (2003). Cochrane has also published novels and slim volumes of short fiction. On Bob Orr, see the note to poem 77.

85: Elizabeth Smither was born in 1941 in New Plymouth, where she still lives. She has published many volumes of poetry, including the award-winning 1989 collection, *A Pattern of Marching*, which contains 'A Cortège of Daughters'. She has published novels, short stories, selections from her journals, and work for children. Her recent poetry collections are *The Lark Quartet* (1999), which won a Montana New Zealand Book Award, and *Red Shoes* (2003), which gathers work from her term as Te Mata Estate New Zealand Poet Laureate. *A Question of Gravity*, which selects work from her last five poetry collections, was published in the United Kingdom in 2004. See http://www.nzepc.auckland.ac.nz/authors/smither/

86: Graham Lindsay (b. 1952) lives in Christchurch but spent many years in Dunedin, where he edited and published the magazine *Morepork*. His first book of poems, *Thousand-Eyed Eel: a sequence of poems from the Maori Land March*, was published in 1975, and his most recent poetry collection, *Lazy Wind Poems*, in 2003. 'Northern Oaks' is a name sometimes used for a small North Dunedin park and sports ground. The poem was first published in *Plainwraps* (1991). See http://www.nzepc.auckland.ac.nz/authors/lindsay/

87: The first book by Virginia Were (b. 1960), *Juliet Bravo Juliet*, was published in 1989 and won the 1990 PEN Best First Book of Poetry Award. A second collection of poetry, *Jump Start*, was published in 1998. She presently lives in Auckland.

88: Jenny Bornholdt was born in 1960 and lives in Wellington. Her first poetry collection, *This Big Face*, was published in 1988. More recently she has published *Miss New Zealand: Selected Poems* (1997), *These Days* (2000) and *Summer (2003)* – the latter a verse record of the year she spent in Menton, France, as Meridian Energy Katherine Mansfield Fellow. With Gregory O'Brien, Bornholdt is co-editor of *My Heart Goes Swimming: New Zealand Love Poems* (1996), and is also an editor of *An Anthology of New Zealand Poetry in English* (1997). In 2005 she was appointed the fifth Te Mata Estate New Zealand Poet Laureate.
See http://www.nzepc.auckland.ac.nz/authors/bornholdt/

89: Alan Riach (b. 1957) came to New Zealand in 1986 from Glasgow to work in the Department of English at Waikato University; he is now professor in the Department of Scottish Literature at Glasgow University, and is editing the works of the Scottish poet Hugh MacDiarmid for publication in the United Kingdom. 'The Blues' is from *This Folding Map* (1990). Other poetry titles include *First and Last Songs* (1995) and *Clearances* (2001).

90: Anne French (b. 1956) won the New Zealand Book Award for Poetry and the Pen Award for First Book of Poetry with *All Cretans are Liars* (1987). 'Cabin Fever' is from her book of the same name, published in 1990. Her most recent collections are *Boys' Night Out* (1999) and *Wild*

(2004). She has worked as an editor and publisher, most notably for Oxford University Press and the Museum of New Zealand Te Papa Tongarewa.

91: Iain Lonie (1932–1988) grew up in Scotland and New Zealand; a noted classical scholar and authority on early medicine, he taught for some years at the University of Otago in Dunedin. His *The Entrance to Purgatory* (1986) was shortlisted for the New Zealand Book Awards; 'Proposal at Allans Beach' is from the posthumous collection, *Winter Walk at Morning* (1991). See http://www.nzepc.auckland.ac.nz/features/dunedin/lonie.asp

92: Bernadette Hall (b. 1945) has published five collections of poetry, and a volume of selected poems, *The Merino Princess* (2004). 'Bowl' is from her 1990 collection, *Of Elephants etc*. Hall has also written a number of works for theatre, and was co-editor of the Canterbury poetry anthology, *Big Sky*. She lives at Amberley Beach, north of Christchurch.
See http://www.nzepc.auckland.ac.nz/authors/hall/

93: Michael Harlow (b. 1937) has published six books of poetry, including *Giotto's Elephant* (1991) where 'No Problem, But Not Easy' appears. In a note Harlow explains that the poem is based on a five-year-old boy's dream reported in a discussion of archetypal images of the mother and the father in Frances G. Wickes's study, *The Inner World of Childhood*. He combines his work as a writer with his practice as a Jungian psychotherapist.
See http://www.nzepc.auckland.ac.nz/authors/harlow/

94: Anne Kennedy (b. 1959) has written fiction (*100 Traditional Smiles*, *Musica Ficta*, *A Boy and His Uncle*) and screenplays, including the adaptation of Dorothy Porter's verse novel, *The Monkey's Mask*. 'I was a Feminist in the Eighties' is from her first book of poems, *Sing-song* (2003), which won a Montana New Zealand Book Award. *Sing-song* is a narrative sequence that records, from the point of view of a mother, the experience of a small girl suffering from eczema.

95: Janet Charman (b. 1954) has published five collections of poetry, most recently *Snowing Down South* (2002). She lives in Auckland, where she works as a teacher. Her work is featured at http://www.nzepc.auckland.ac.nz/authors/charman/

96: Margaret Mahy (b. 1936) trained and worked as a librarian but is now a full-time writer, living in a house she partly built herself at Governors Bay, near Lyttelton. Twice the winner of the Carnegie Medal and a four-time winner of the Esther Glen Award, she has an international reputation as a children's writer, chiefly for her fiction. A book of essays and interviews, *A Dissolving Ghost*, was published in 2000, and her essay *Notes of a Bag Lady* was published in 2003. 'Bubble Trouble' is from *Bubble Trouble and Other Poems and Stories* (London, 1991).

97: 'Fast Cold' is from Forbes Williams's first book of stories, *Motel View*, published in 1992. Williams was born in 1960 and lives in Dunedin, where he has taught at the University of Otago Medical School.

98: 'How to Talk' is the title poem of Andrew Johnston's first poetry collection (1993), which won the New Zealand Book Award for Poetry. There have been two subsequent poetry collections, *The Sounds* (1996) and *Birds of Europe* (2000); a selection of poems, *The Open Window*, was published in the United Kingdom in 1999. Johnston was born in Upper Hutt in 1963, and now lives in Paris where he works for the *International Herald Tribune* and edits the website http://thepage.name/. There is more information about his own poetry at http://andrewjohnston.org/

99: Damien Wilkins (b. 1963) grew up in the Hutt Valley and came to prominence after winning an award for his first book-length work of fiction, *The Veteran Perils* (1990). After studying in the United States, where he received a Whiting Award, he returned to New Zealand in 1992. His novel *The Miserables* (1993) won the New Zealand Book Award for Fiction. More recent novels are *Little Masters* (1996), *Nineteen Widows Under Ash* (2000) and *Chemistry* (2002). 'My Father's Stutter' is from Wilkins's sole poetry collection *The Idles* (1993).

100: This is the final poem in *Voices*, a sequence of historical monologues published by C.K. Stead in 1990. Stead was born in 1932; he was for some time Professor of English at Auckland University but has for many years worked as a full-time writer. He has produced many volumes of poetry since his first collection, *Whether the Will is Free*, was published in 1962. He is also the author of novels, collections of short stories and several volumes of literary criticism.

101: Stephen Sinclair (b. 1956) has had considerable success as a playwright and screenwriter – he co-wrote *Meet the Feebles* and *Braindead* with Fran Walsh and Peter Jackson and contributed, too, to the *Lord of the Rings* screenplays – and has also published fiction for children and adults. 'The Historian' appears in his recent book of verse, *The Dwarf and the Stripper* (2003).

102: Stephanie de Montalk (b. 1945) included 'Concrete' in her first book, *Animals Indoors* (2000), which won the Jessie Mackay Best First Book Award for Poetry. A second collection, *The Scientific Evidence of Dr Wang*, was published in 2002, and a third is forthcoming. Her biography of her eccentric cousin, the poet Geoffrey de Montalk, was published in 2001 in New Zealand – and more recently in Poland (in translation).

103: John Clarke (b. 1948) released this song (in his Fred Dagg persona) in 1975; this text is from the 1988 re-release. Clarke was born and educated in New Zealand, but has lived in Australia since 1977, where he is well-known as a comedian and political satirist. The television series *The Games* is a notable recent achievement, while he has also published some fine verse parodies, most recently *The Even More Complete Book of Australian Verse* (2004). An entirely fictional publication, attributed to him in one of his author notes, is *Both New Zealand Poets* (1981).

104: Robert Sullivan (b. 1967) is of Ngapuhi and Irish descent. His books of poetry are *Jazz Waiata* (1990), *Piki Ake* (1993), *Star Waka* (1999) and *Captain Cook in the Underworld* (2002). With Albert Wendt and Reina Whaitiri, he edited the award-winning *Whetu Moana: Contemporary Polynesian Poems in English* (2003). He trained and has worked as a librarian but presently teaches at the University of Hawaii in Honolulu. 'Waka 99' is from the 100-poem, 2001-line sequence *Star Waka*. The author's note reads: 'I wrote *Star Waka* with some threads to it: that each poem must have a star, a waka or the ocean. This sequence is like a waka, members of the crew change, the rhythm and the view changes – it is subject to the laws of nature.'
See http://www.nzepc.auckland.ac.nz/authors/sullivan/

105: David Geary (b. 1963) is best-known as a playwright – *Pack of Girls* (unpublished, 1991), *Lovelock's Dream Run* (1993) and *The Learner's Stand* (unpublished, 1995) – but he is also the author of a book of linked short stories, *A Man of the People*, published in 2003. 'Marton' is reprinted from *Sport* 18 (1997).

106: Jo Randerson (b. 1973) is best known as an innovative writer, director and performer in the world of New Zealand theatre, but she is also the author of distinctive works for the page that often have the flavour of parable or fable. 'Why Our Washing Machine Broke' is from her 2000 book, *The Spit Children*. Other titles are *The Knot* and, more recently, *The Keys to Hell*.

107: Kapka Kassabova (b. 1973) was born in Bulgaria, and came to New Zealand with her parents in 1992. 'Security' was originally printed, in a slightly different version, as part of a larger sequence in her first book, *All Roads Lead to the Sea* (1997), which won the Jessie Mackay Best First Book Award for Poetry. She has published a further book of poems, *Dismemberment* (1998), and two novels. This text is taken from *Someone Else's Life* (published in the United Kingdom and New Zealand, 2003), which prints new poems alongside work from her first two collections.

108: Vivienne Plumb (b. 1955) has been a professional actor in Australia and New Zealand, but is now a full-time writer. She has published an award-winning collection of stories, *The Wife Who Spoke Japanese in her Sleep* (1993), and longer fiction including the novel *Secret City* (2003). Her three collections of poetry are *Salamanca* (1998), *Avalanche* (2000) and *Nefarious* (2004). 'The Tank' won the 1998 NZ Poetry Society International Poetry Competition and is collected in *Avalanche*. Bats is a Wellington theatre.

109: Gregory O'Brien (b. 1960) is a painter and art curator as well as a poet, editor and essayist. He is the author of *Hotere – Out the Black Window* (1997) and *Welcome to the South Seas* (2004), an introduction to New Zealand art for children. He is co-editor of *An Anthology of New Zealand Poetry in English* (1997). His collection of essays, *After Bathing at Baxter's*, was published in 2002. His most recent books of poetry are *Winter I Was* (1999) and *Afternoon of an Evening Train* (2005), where 'Ode to the Waihi Beach Dump', first written in January 2000, is collected.

110: Emma Neale (b. 1969) lives in Dunedin where she works as a freelance editor and writer. She has published three novels. Her two collections of poetry are *Sleeve Notes* (1999) and *How to Make a Million* (2002). Neale edited the anthology *Creative Juices* (2001) and the 2004 issue of the on-line annual *Best New Zealand Poems* (http://www.vuw.ac.nz/modernletters/bnzp/).

111: Laura Ranger (b. 1984) lives in Wellington, and began writing poems when she was six. After 'Two Word Poem' appeared in *100 New Zealand Poems* in 1993, there was a collection of her work – *Laura's Poems* (1995) – which became a best-seller. She subsequently attended Poetry International in Rotterdam in 1997.

112: Anna Jackson (b. 1967) has published three collections of poetry: *The Long Road to Teatime* (2000), *The Pastoral Kitchen* (2001) and *Catullus for Children* (2003), where 'Fontanello' is printed. She lectures in the Department of English at Victoria University of Wellington.

113: Rhian Gallagher was born in Timaru in 1961, but has lived in London since about 1990. 'The Quiet Place' is from her first book of poems, *Salt Water Creek*, which was published in London in 2003 and was shortlisted for the Forward Prize for First Collection.

114: Chris Price (b. 1962) has been a publisher and was, for seven years, editor of *Landfall*; she now teaches in the creative writing programme at Victoria University. 'Dog's Body' is from her book, *Husk* (2002), which won the Jessie Mackay Best First Book Award for Poetry.

115: Tusiata Avia was born in Christchurch in 1966, and is of Samoan descent through her father. Many of her poems explore the Polynesian dimensions of her heritage. 'Wild Dogs Under My Skirt' is the title poem of her first collection, which was published in 2004. 'Tufuga': master tattooist. A note by the author reads: 'The fourth stanza refers to the traditional Samoan story of the octopus and the rat. The rat tricked the octopus into letting him ride on his head from one island to another. During the free ride the rat shit on the octopus' head.'

116: Glenn Colquhoun (b. 1964) is a doctor and a poet. His first collection of poetry, *The Art of Walking Upright* (1999), won the Jessie Mackay Best First Book Award for Poetry. 'Communion' is from a larger sequence in his 2002 collection, *Playing God*, which explores the medical dimensions of its title. Glenn Colquhoun received the Prize in Modern Letters in 2004. He has also published the essay *Jumping Ship* (2004), and two books for children.

117: Rachel Bush (b. 1941) lives in Nelson, where for many years she worked as a teacher. Her first book, *The Hungry Woman*, was published in 1997. 'The Strong Mothers' is from *The Unfortunate Singer*, published in 2002.

118: James Brown was indeed born in Palmerston North, in 1966. His poem was first published in the on-line magazine *Turbine* (http://www.vuw.ac.nz/turbine/). He now lives in Wellington and works as a freelance editor and writer. His poetry collections are *Go Round Power, Please* (1995), which won the Jessie Mackay Best First Book Award for Poetry, *Lemon* (1999) and

Favourite Monsters (2002). Brown has also published *Instructions for Poetry Readings* under the pseudonym Dr Ernest M Bluespire. The booklet is composed of wise if sometimes dangerous advice for those wishing to give or attend poetry readings.

119: Kate Camp (b. 1972) won the Jessie Mackay Best First Book Award for Poetry with *Unfamiliar Legends of the Stars* (1998). Her second collection *Realia*, where 'Documentaries', is collected, was published in 2001; a third book is forthcoming. She has also published the essay, *On Kissing*, but may be best known for 'Kate's Klassics' on National Radio.

120: Sonja Yelich was born in 1965 in Auckland, where she lives with her partner and four children. '1YA' is from her first solo book of poems, *Clung*, published in 2004. Her work was also published with that of Jane Gardner and Stu Bagby in *AUP New Poets 2* (2002).

121: Adrian Croucher was born in 1969 in Auckland, where he has mostly lived. He has worked as a scientist, and as a musician with percussion ensemble *From Scratch*, and started writing fairly recently. 'Nowhere' was first published in the December 2004 issue of *Staple* magazine.

Listings of publications by many of the writers in this anthology can be found at: http://www.library.auckland.ac.nz/subjects/nzp/nzlit2/authors_az.htm

The New Zealand Book Council's writers' site is also invaluable: http://www.bookcouncil.org.nz/writers/index.html

Other anthologies that will supplement this collection are: for early New Zealand poetry, Harvey McQueen's *The New Place: The Poetry of Settlement in New Zealand 1852–1914* (1993); for poetry by Maori and Pacific Island writers, *Whetu Moana: Contemporary Polynesian Poems in English* (2003); for poetry by women, Lydia Wevers's *Yellow Pencils* (1988); for poetry of the sixties and seventies, *Big Smoke*, edited by Alan Brunton, Murray Edmond and Michele Leggott (2000). The most comprehensive in-print anthology is the 1997 *An Anthology of New Zealand Poetry*, edited by Jenny Bornholdt, Gregory O'Brien and Mark Williams.

The annual *Best New Zealand Poems* website selects work from magazines and poetry collections published in each calendar year: http://www.vuw.ac.nz/modernletters/bnzp/

The New Zealand Electronic Poetry Centre is a significant resource, not only for information about a number of the writers included in this anthology but also for essays, interviews, and other on-line information about New Zealand poetry: http://www.nzepc.auckland.ac.nz/

Interviews with a number of the poets published here are printed in *In the Same Room: Conversations with New Zealand Writers*, edited by Elizabeth Alley and Mark Williams (1992); *Moments of Invention: Portraits of 21 New Zealand Writers*, Greg O'Brien and Robert Cross (1988); and *Talking about Ourselves: Twelve New Zealand Poets in Conversation with Harry Ricketts* (1982).

acknowledgements

2 Cilla McQueen; 4: Chris Orsman; 9: Fiona Farrell, Auckland University Press (AUP); 10: Ruth Dallas; 12: W.H. Oliver; 15: Dinah Hawken, Victoria University Press (VUP); 17: Peter Bland; 23: Kevin Ireland, AUP; 24: Lloyd Jones, Penguin Books (NZ) Ltd; 25: University of Canterbury Library; 26: John Gallas, from *Star City*, Carcanet Press, 2004; 28: VUP; 29: R.A.K. Mason Literary Trust; 30: Hamish McCarroll; 32: Pia Glover and the Denis Glover Estate; 33: Janis Fairburn, A.R.D. Fairburn Literary Trust; 34: Bub Bridger, Mallinson Rendel Publishers; 35: Alan Roddick, The Estate of Charles Brasch; 37: Derek Challis, the Estate of Robin Hyde; 39: Permission to include 'A Note on the Russian War' by Janet Frame, courtesy of the copyright owner, the Janet Frame Literary Trust, Dunedin; 42: Alexandra Smithyman, AUP; 43: Rachel McAlpine; 45: Robyn Matheson; 46: Hone Tuwhare; 47: Mrs M.J. Joseph; 49: Keith Sinclair, AUP; 50: Cecilia Johnson; 51: Margaret Edgecumbe, AUP; 52: Fleur Adcock; 53: Vincent O'Sullivan, VUP; 54: Alistair Campbell, AUP; 55: Mrs J.C. Baxter; 56: David Mitchell; 57: Peter Olds; 58: Sam Hunt; 59: Ian Wedde; 61: Rore Hapipi; 62: Murray Edmond; 63: Michael Jackson; 64: Wystan Curnow; 65: Apirana Taylor; 66: Jeny Curnow, Tim Curnow and Elizabeth Caffin, AUP; 67: Frances Edmond, Lauris Edmond's 'The Names' from *Selected Poems* 1975-2000, Bridget Williams Books, 2001; 68: Keri Hulme; 69: Iain Sharp; 71: John Newton; 72: Hugh Lauder; 74: Elizabeth Nannestad, AUP; 75: Amber McWilliams; 76: Michael Morrissey, AUP; 77: Bob Orr, AUP; 78: Meg Campbell; 79: Owen Marshall; 80: Roma Potiki; 81: David Eggleton, Penguin; 82: Michele Leggott, AUP; 83: Brian Turner; 84: Geoff Cochrane, VUP; 85: Elizabeth Smither, AUP; 86: Graham Lindsay; 87: Virginia Were, VUP; 88: Jenny Bornholdt, VUP; 89: Alan Riach, AUP; 90: Anne French, AUP; 91: Bridie Lonie; 92: Bernadette Hall; 93: Michael Harlow; 94: Anne Kennedy, AUP; 95: Janet Charman, AUP; 96: Margaret Mahy; 97: Forbes Williams, VUP; 98: Andrew Johnston, VUP; 99: Damien Wilkins, VUP; 100: C.K. Stead; 101: Stephen Sinclair; 102: Stephanie de Montalk, VUP; 103: John Clarke; 104: Robert Sullivan, AUP; 105: David Geary; 106: Jo Randerson, VUP; 107: Kapka Kassabova, AUP; 108: Vivienne Plumb; 109: Gregory O'Brien, VUP; 110: Emma Neale; 111: Laura Ranger; 112: Anna Jackson, AUP; 113: Rhian Gallagher, Enitharmon Press; 114: Chris Price, AUP; 115: Tusiata Avia, VUP; 116: Glenn Colquhoun, Steele Roberts Publications Ltd; 117: Rachel Bush, VUP; 118: James Brown; 119: Kate Camp, VUP; 120: Sonja Yelich, AUP; 121: Adrian Croucher.

Every effort was made to contact all other copyright holders not included in this list.

Thanks for their assistance to Katie Hardwick-Smith, the staff of the Alexander Turnbull Library and the Beaglehole Room at Victoria University, and to friends for their suggestions.

index of authors

ADAMS, Arthur H.	13	EDMOND, Murray	62
ADCOCK, Fleur	52	EGGLESTON, Kim	73
ALLAN, Florence E.	60	EGGLETON, David	81
AVIA, Tusiata	115	FAIRBURN, A.R.D.	33
BARR, John	8	FARRELL, Fiona	9
BAUGHAN, Blanche	21	FITZGERALD, James Edward	7
BAXTER, James K.	55	FOSTER, Glennis	70
BETHELL, Ursula	28	FRAME, Janet	39
BLAND, Peter	17	FRENCH, Anne	90
BORNHOLDT, Jenny	88	GALLAGHER, Rhian	113
BRACKEN, Thomas	16	GALLAS, John	26
BRASCH, Charles	35	GEARY, David	105
BRIDGER, Bub	34	GLOVER, Denis	32
BROWN, James	118	HALL, Bernadette	92
BUSH, Rachel	117	HAPIPI, Rore	61
CAMP, Kate	119	HARLOW, Michael	93
CAMPBELL, Alistair Te Ariki	54	HART-SMITH, William	41
CAMPBELL, Meg	78	HAWKEN, Dinah	15
CAPE, Peter	44	HERVEY, J.R.	36
CHARLES, Joe	45	HODGSON, William Charles	19
CHARMAN, Janet	95	HULME, Keri	68
CLARKE, John	103	HUNT, Sam	58
COCHRANE, Geoff	84	HYDE, Robin	37
COLQUHOUN, Glenn	116	IRELAND, Kevin	23
CROUCHER, Adrian	121	JACKSON, Anna	112
CURNOW, Allen	66	JACKSON, Michael	63
CURNOW, Wystan	64	JOHNSON, Louis	50
CURRIE, Una	31	JOHNSTON, Andrew	98
DALLAS, Ruth	10	JONES, Lloyd	24
DE MONTALK, Stephanie	102	JOSEPH, M.K.	47
DUGGAN, Eileen	30	KASSABOVA, Kapka	107
EDMOND, Lauris	67	KENNEDY, Anne	94

LAUDER, Hugh	72		SINCLAIR, Keith	49
LAWSON, Henry	22		SINCLAIR, Stephen	101
LEGGOTT, Michele	82		SMITHER, Elizabeth	85
LINDSAY, Graham	86		SMITHYMAN, Kendrick	51
LONIE, Iain	91		STANLEY, Mary	42
MACKAY, Jessie	11		STEAD, C.K.	100
MAHY, Margaret	96		STRONACH, Bruce	40
MANSFIELD, Katherine	27		SULLIVAN, Robert	104
MARSHALL, Owen	79		TAYLOR, Apirana	65
MASON, R.A.K.	29		TURNER, Brian	83
MCALPINE, Rachel	43		TUWHARE, Hone	46
MCDONALD, Donald	38		WALL, Arnold	25
MCQUEEN, Cilla	2		WEDDE, Ian	59
MCWILLIAMS, Amber	75		WERE, Virginia	87
MITCHELL, David	56		WILKINS, Damien	99
MORRISSEY, Michael	76		WILLIAMS, Forbes	97
NANNESTAD, Elizabeth	74		WILSON, Anne Glenny	18
NEALE, Emma	110		WRIGHT, David McKee	14
NEWTON, John	71		YELICH, Sonja	120
O'BRIEN, Gregory	109			
O'SULLIVAN, Vincent	53			
OLDS, Peter	57			
OLIVER, W.H.	12			
ORR, Bob	77			
ORSMAN, Chris	4			
PLUMB, Vivienne	108			
POTIKI, Roma	80			
PRICE, Chris	114			
RANDERSON, Jo	106			
RANGER, Laura	111			
RIACH, Alan	89			
SATCHELL, William	20			
SHARP, Iain	69			